GLOBAL VIEWPOINTS

Adoption

Other Books of Related Interest:

At Issue Series

Are Adoption Policies Fair?

Introducing Issues with Opposing Viewpoints Series

Adoption

Issues That Concern You Series

Adoption

Teen Parenting

Adoption

Diane Andrews Henningfeld, Book Editor

GREENHAVEN PRESS
A part of Gale, Cengage Learning

GALE
CENGAGE Learning

Detroit • New York • San Francisco • New Haven, Conn • Waterville, Maine • London

Elizabeth Des Chenes, *Director, Publishing Solutions*

© 2013 Greenhaven Press, a part of Gale, Cengage Learning

Gale and Greenhaven Press are registered trademarks used herein under license.

For more information, contact:
Greenhaven Press
27500 Drake Rd.
Farmington Hills, MI 48331-3535
Or you can visit our Internet site at gale.cengage.com

For product information and technology assistance, contact us at

Gale Customer Support, 1-800-877-4253
For permission to use material from this text or product, submit all requests online at www.cengage.com/permissions

Further permissions questions can be emailed to permissionrequest@cengage.com

Articles in Greenhaven Press anthologies are often edited for length to meet page requirements. In addition, original titles of these works are changed to clearly present the main thesis and to explicitly indicate the author's opinion. Every effort is made to ensure that Greenhaven Press accurately reflects the original intent of the authors. Every effort has been made to trace the owners of copyrighted material.

Cover image © Andrea Laurita/Vetta/Getty Images.

LIBRARY OF CONGRESS CATALOGING-IN-PUBLICATION DATA

Adoption / Diane Andrews Henningfeld, Book Editor.
    pages cm. -- (Global viewpoints)
    Includes bibliographical references and index.
    ISBN 978-0-7377-6259-4 (hbk.) -- ISBN 978-0-7377-6435-2 (pbk.)
    1. Adoption. I. Henningfeld, Diane Andrews.
    HV875.A3176 2013
    362.734--dc23

                                                        2012032403

Printed in Mexico
1 2 3 4 5 6 7 16 15 14 13

Contents

During the so-called "Sixties Scoop," Canadian aid agencies removed thousands of First Nations children from their homes to be adopted by white parents; now adults, some of these children are suing the Canadian government for the loss of their culture as a wrongful act.

Chapter 4: The Rights of Adoptive Parents, Birth Parents, and Adoptees

Koreans who were adopted abroad have returned to Seoul to reform adoption law and to persuade the government to encourage Korean families to stay together rather than send their children to foreign families for adoption.

Foreword

"The problems of all of humanity can only be solved by all of humanity."
—Swiss author Friedrich Dürrenmatt

Global interdependence has become an undeniable reality. Mass media and technology have increased worldwide access to information and created a society of global citizens. Understanding and navigating this global community is a challenge, requiring a high degree of information literacy and a new level of learning sophistication.

Building on the success of its flagship series, Opposing Viewpoints, Greenhaven Press has created the Global Viewpoints series to examine a broad range of current, often controversial topics of worldwide importance from a variety of international perspectives. Providing students and other readers with the information they need to explore global connections and think critically about worldwide implications, each Global Viewpoints volume offers a panoramic view of a topic of widespread significance.

Drugs, famine, immigration—a broad, international treatment is essential to do justice to social, environmental, health, and political issues such as these. Junior high, high school, and early college students, as well as general readers, can all use Global Viewpoints anthologies to discern the complexities relating to each issue. Readers will be able to examine unique national perspectives while, at the same time, appreciating the interconnectedness that global priorities bring to all nations and cultures.

Material in each volume is selected from a diverse range of sources, including journals, magazines, newspapers, nonfiction books, speeches, government documents, pamphlets, organization newsletters, and position papers. Global Viewpoints is truly global, with material drawn primarily from international sources available in English and secondarily from US sources with extensive international coverage.

Features of each volume in the Global Viewpoints series include:

- An **annotated table of contents** that provides a brief summary of each essay in the volume, including the name of the country or area covered in the essay.

- An **introduction** specific to the volume topic.

- A **world map** to help readers locate the countries or areas covered in the essays.

- For each viewpoint, an **introduction** that contains notes about the author and source of the viewpoint explains why material from the specific country is being presented, summarizes the main points of the viewpoint, and offers three **guided reading questions** to aid in understanding and comprehension.

- **For further discussion** questions that promote critical thinking by asking the reader to compare and contrast aspects of the viewpoints or draw conclusions about perspectives and arguments.

- A worldwide list of **organizations to contact** for readers seeking additional information.

- A **periodical bibliography** for each chapter and a **bibliography of books** on the volume topic to aid in further research.

- A comprehensive **subject index** to offer access to people, places, events, and subjects cited in the text, with the countries covered in the viewpoints highlighted.

Global Viewpoints is designed for a broad spectrum of readers who want to learn more about current events, history, political science, government, international relations, economics, environmental science, world cultures, and sociology—students doing research for class assignments or debates, teachers and faculty seeking to supplement course materials, and others wanting to understand current issues better. By presenting how people in various countries perceive the root causes, current consequences, and proposed solutions to worldwide challenges, Global Viewpoints volumes offer readers opportunities to enhance their global awareness and their knowledge of cultures worldwide.

Introduction

> *"Adoption history illustrates that public and private issues are inseparable. Ideas about blood and belonging, nature and nurture, needs and rights are not the exclusive products of individual choices and personal freedoms."*
>
> —*Ellen Herman,*
> *Adoption History Project,*
> *University of Oregon,*
> *February 24, 2012*

Historically, most countries and most cultures have had provisions for children whose parents are either unwilling or unable to care for them. Written evidence exists that as far back as the Babylonian Empire, parentless children were subject to adoption by relatives or other adults in the culture. Usually such arrangements benefitted the adopter rather than the adoptee, usually in the form of financial gain. In poorer families, the motivation for adoption could be to increase the labor force represented by the family. If a couple had no son to help work the land, for example, they might attempt to adopt one to provide labor and increase the family's likelihood of survival.

Adoption to benefit the child came much later; according to Ellen Herman of the Adoption History Project at the University of Oregon, "Adoption's close association with humanitarianism, upward mobility, and infertility, however, are uniquely modern phenomena." The new attention to the humanitarian aspect of adoption resulted in projects such as the Orphan Train Movement. In 1854 the Children's Aid Society and the New York Foundling Hospital decided that something must be done about the estimated thirty thousand homeless children roaming the streets of New York City, according to the National Orphan Train Complex, a museum and research center. The two organizations began a program that moved some three hundred thousand children out of the city of New York to families in forty-seven states and Canada, transporting them by train.

In addition, in the United States the philosophy that adoption should benefit the child led to legalization and regulation of the process to try to ensure that children were well matched with their adoptive families. Herman notes that the first modern adoption law was the Massachusetts Adoption of Children Act, passed in 1851. Many developed countries in the West did not begin to regulate adoptions until the twentieth century, however. In the United Kingdom, for example, adoption became legalized in 1920, according to Lisa Harker, writing for BBC News.

At times adoptions played a role in a larger political agenda, according to many scholars such as Matthew L.M. Fletcher in *American Indian Education: Counternarratives in Racism, Struggle, and the Law.* In the United States, Canada, and Australia, for example, many indigenous children were taken from their birth families and were either sent to boarding schools or adopted by white families. In Australia, these children are now called "the stolen generations." Although in these countries adoption officials argued that they were acting for the benefit of the children by placing them in families with higher standards of living, it is now widely acknowledged that the underlying belief behind the adoptions was assimilation. That is, by assimilating these children into white culture, the government could solve the so-called "Indian problem." The Australian government's Law Reform Commission, for example, in explaining the history of the adoption of Aboriginal peoples, writes,

> In the 1950s 'assimilation' became a widely accepted goal for all Aboriginal people and was adopted as policy by the Com-

monwealth and by all State Governments. The policy was defined at the 1961 Native Welfare Conference of Federal and State Ministers in these terms:

The policy of assimilation means that all Aborigines and part-Aborigines are expected to attain the same manner of living as other Australians and to live as members of a single Australian community, enjoying the same rights and privileges, accepting the same customs and influenced by the same beliefs as other Australians.

The number of adoptions in the United States and other Western nations peaked around 1970. Since that time, the adoption rate has fallen for a number of reasons: First, the stigma attached to single parenthood has gradually been erased in these countries and many single mothers now choose to keep their babies; and second, in vitro fertilization has addressed fertility problems for many couples. Others would argue that the bureaucracy and long waiting period associated with the adoption process discourage adoptive parents. Some would-be adoptive parents have turned to international adoptions as a way around the shortage of domestic babies for adoption. Nevertheless, international adoptions can sometimes be conducted in unethical and potentially abusive ways, causing harm to the children and the birth families. In some instances, children are even stolen and sold to adoption agencies. To address these problems, many countries have joined the Hague Convention on Protection of Children and Cooperation in Respect of Intercountry Adoption, also known as the Hague Adoption Convention, an agreement that establishes ethical standards for adoption among all member nations.

Today, at first consideration, adopting a child seems to be a selfless and altruistic action. A child whose parents are unable to care for him or her needs a home and finds a loving family through the goodness of adoptive parents. As the passages above indicate, however, adoption is a process that can be fraught with conflict and the potential to violate the basic human rights of the child, the birth parents, and the adoptive parents. In many cases, adoption is a wonderful, loving process, one that creates a new family wherein all members benefit. In other cases, adoptions are not handled ethically, birth mothers are coerced into giving up their children, or children end up in abusive situations. There are no easy answers, and there are many beliefs surrounding adoptions. The chapters in *Global Viewpoints: Adoption* offer insights on adoption around the world, on the joys and dangers of transnational adoption, on racial and indigenous issues of adoption, on the role of gender in adoption, and finally on the rights of all parties.

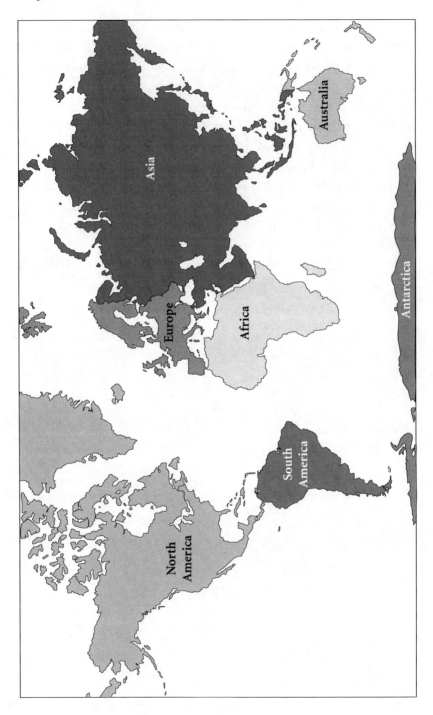

GLOBALVIEWPOINTS

Adoption Worldwide

Child Adoption Trends and Policies Worldwide: An Overview

Department of Economic and Social Affairs of the United Nations (DESA)

In the following viewpoint, the Department of Economic and Social Affairs of the United Nations (DESA) summarizes the findings of a study of adoption practices among member nations. DESA notes that adoption rights for children and parents differ considerably among nations, domestic adoptions are more common than international adoptions, the AIDS epidemic has left many orphans in need of adoption, and many nations do not keep accurate records or statistics concerning adoption—making it difficult to draw conclusions from the data. DESA is the United Nations branch charged with eradicating poverty, improving gender rights, and working on climate change, among other responsibilities.

As you read, consider the following questions:

1. How many countries do not have legal provisions allowing child adoption, according to the viewpoint?

2. As reported in the viewpoint, in how many countries are single persons allowed to adopt?

Department of Economic and Social Affairs of the United Nations (DESA), "Executive Summary," *Child Adoption: Trends and Policies*, DESA, United Nations, 2009, pp. xv–xix. Copyright © 2009 by the United Nations. All rights reserved. Reproduced by permission.

3. What percentage of children are adopted at age five or younger worldwide, according to the viewpoint?

Adoption is one of the oldest social institutions. Nevertheless, adoption still raises highly emotive issues because of its fundamental implications for the meaning of familial ties. Questions on whether adoption serves the best interests of children, who should be allowed to adopt and the role of governments in regulating such decisions are frequent subjects of debate. Yet, despite the heightened attention to these issues, much of the information on adoption remains anecdotal. Data on the number of children adopted domestically are rarely available and when they are, they tend to be out of date. Similarly, comparable information on trends in intercountry adoptions—that is, adoptions that involve a change of country of residence for the adopted person—is often lacking or is available for just a few countries. . . .

Understanding adoption policies and their origins is all the more important today because, as adoption has become global, inconsistencies among the legal principles and traditions regarding adoption in different countries are increasingly coming to the fore. The major findings of this study are summarized below.

Facts About Adoption Worldwide

1. *There are over a quarter of a million adoptions every year.* The United Nations Population Division estimates that some 260,000 children are adopted each year. This estimate implies that fewer than 12 children are adopted for every 100,000 persons under age 18. Adoption remains, therefore, a relatively rare event.

2. *A few countries account for most adoptions.* The United States of America, with over 127,000 adoptions in 2001, accounts for nearly half of the total number of adoptions world-

wide. Large numbers of adoptions also take place in China (almost 46,000 in 2001) and in the Russian Federation (more than 23,000 in 2001).

3. *The purpose of adoption has evolved over time.* Historically, adoption occurred primarily to preserve and transmit family lines or inheritance, to gain political power or to forge alliances between families. Adopted persons were usually adolescents or adults who could guarantee the continuation of the family line. The notion that adoption was a means for promoting children's welfare did not take hold until the midnineteenth century. Today, the principle of ensuring that the best interests of the child are served by adoption is the paramount consideration enshrined in most adoption laws.

4. *Over 160 countries recognize the legal institution of adoption, but 20 countries do not have legal provisions allowing child adoption.* In most of the countries where adoption is not possible, alternative procedures such as guardianship or the placement of children under the care of relatives are permitted. Religion often plays a key role in determining the conditions under which such alternative practices may be pursued.

5. *In some countries, informal adoption and fostering are perceived as preferable to formal adoption.* Informal or *de facto* adoption and fostering are practices that allow parents to put children in the care of others (usually relatives) without having to cut all ties with their children. These practices contrast markedly with the secrecy and finality that have come to characterize adoption in the Western context.

Today, the principle of ensuring that the best interests of the child are served by adoption is the paramount consideration enshrined in most adoption laws.

Requirements and Rights

6. *The consequences of an adoption for the rights of adopted children differ considerably among countries.* In some countries,

adopted children acquire the same rights as birth children, including the right to inheritance, and adopted children sever all legal ties with their birth parents. In other countries, the termination of natural ties between birth parents and children is viewed as culturally unacceptable.

7. *Requirements for prospective adoptive parents vary considerably among countries.* In 81 countries, adoption laws establish a minimum age for prospective adoptive parents and in 15 countries, adoption laws also stipulate a maximum age. Single persons are allowed to adopt in 100 countries but in 15, only married couples can adopt. In many countries, laws have been amended to allow older persons or single persons to adopt. However, in some cases, the criteria that potential adoptive parents must meet have become more stringent. Adoption by stepparents, for instance, is currently discouraged in several countries because of the potentially detrimental effects that such adoptions are deemed to have on the child's relationship to his or her noncustodial biological parent. The requirements for intercountry adoptions have also been tightened in several countries of origin.

The United States, France, and Spain, in order of importance, are the major countries of destination of children adopted internationally.

---

8. *Domestic adoptions far outnumber intercountry adoptions.* Almost 85 per cent of all adoptions involve citizens or residents of the same country. Domestic adoptions represent at least half of all adoptions in 57 of the 96 countries with data. Whereas the number of domestic adoptions has been declining in many developed countries, several developing countries have experienced an increase in the number of domestic adoptions, partly because of the implementation of policies to encourage local residents to adopt.

9. *Adoptions by stepparents and other relatives account for more than half of all domestic adoptions.* Nevertheless, the number of adoptions by stepparents and other relatives has been declining in recent years. In some countries, the introduction of legislation discouraging adoptions by stepparents accounts partly for this trend. Declining remarriage rates and an increasing prevalence of informal parenting arrangements are also contributing to that decline.

Intercountry Adoption

10. *The number of intercountry adoptions has been increasing.* Both the number of intercountry adoptions and their share among all adoptions have been increasing. In many European countries, intercountry adoptions now account for more than half of all adoptions.

11. *The United States, France and Spain, in order of importance, are the major countries of destination of children adopted internationally.* Other countries that experience large inflows of children adopted from abroad are Canada, Germany, Italy, the Netherlands and Sweden. Each of these countries has recorded over 1,000 foreign adoptions annually in recent years.

12. *Asian and East European countries are the major sources of children adopted through an intercountry procedure.* Relatively few children adopted internationally originate in Africa or Latin America and the Caribbean. The countries of origin accounting for most international adoptions are China, Guatemala, the Republic of Korea, the Russian Federation and Ukraine. More than half of the children adopted abroad originate in those five countries.

13. *The dwindling supply of children available for domestic adoption may partially explain the increase in the number of intercountry adoptions.* In developed countries, the widespread availability of reliable, safe and inexpensive contraception has meant that there are fewer children available for adoption. In addition, wider societal acceptance of single parenthood and

the greater availability of welfare support have meant that fewer single mothers give up their children for adoption.

14. *The characteristics of children available for domestic adoption has also contributed to the increase in the number of intercountry adoptions.* Adoptable children within countries are often older than those desired by adoptive parents. The desire for younger children has probably prompted some parents to adopt children abroad. Intercountry adoptions are also favoured in contexts where adoption procedures are less demanding and faster for intercountry adoptions than for domestic adoption.

Age and Gender Considerations

15. *Over 60 per cent of adopted children are under age five at the time of adoption.* Despite adoptive parents' preference for younger children, relatively few adoptions involve children under age one. Adoptions of children older than five years also tend to be rare and, when they occur, they frequently involve stepchildren.

16. *In countries of destination, children adopted domestically tend to be older than children adopted through an intercountry procedure.* This outcome results, at least in part, from the fact that domestic adoptions comprise a larger proportion of stepchild adoptions, which usually involve older children. The preference of prospective adoptive parents for adopting younger children may also be a factor. In countries of origin, children adopted domestically tend to be younger than those adopted by foreign parents through an intercountry procedure. The principle of subsidiarity, whereby intercountry adoption is considered only after all other options have been exhausted, may be the reason for this difference.

17. *More girls are adopted than boys.* In both domestic and intercountry adoptions, the number of girls adopted exceeds that of boys. In some countries, this pattern is associated with imbalances in the sex distribution of children available for

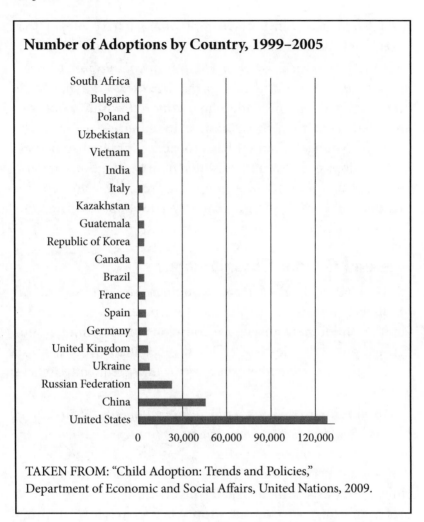

Number of Adoptions by Country, 1999–2005

South Africa
Bulgaria
Poland
Uzbekistan
Vietnam
India
Italy
Kazakhstan
Guatemala
Republic of Korea
Canada
Brazil
France
Spain
Germany
United Kingdom
Ukraine
Russian Federation
China
United States

0   30,000   60,000   90,000   120,000

TAKEN FROM: "Child Adoption: Trends and Policies,"
Department of Economic and Social Affairs, United Nations, 2009.

adoption. In other countries, the perception that girls are easier to raise or that female children are more likely to provide assistance with housework or caregiving activities may explain in part the higher percentage of adoptions involving girls.

18. *Most adoptive parents are in the 30–44 age group.* Adoptions by parents who are younger than 30 or older than 44 are less frequent, partly because of the maximum and minimum age limits imposed by the legislation of most countries. Fe-

male adoptive parents are generally younger, partly because they are less likely to adopt as stepparents.

19. *The number of male adoptive parents is roughly the same as that of female adoptive parents.* However, in countries with large numbers of adoptions by stepparents or where adoption by single persons is permitted, differences by sex are noticeable. Among adopting stepparents, men outnumber women, but women outnumber men among single persons who adopt.

The perception that girls are easier to raise or that female children are more likely to provide assistance with housework or caregiving activities may explain in part the higher percentage of adoptions involving girls.

Other Factors Affecting Adoption

20. *People who are unable to achieve their desired family size through childbearing often resort to adoption.* Country-level surveys and ethnographic studies indicate that persons who are involuntarily childless as a result of sterility, subfecundity or other factors often seek to adopt.

21. *Adoption is not simply a demographic response to achieve a desired family size for those suffering from involuntary sterility and subfecundity.* Whereas involuntary childlessness is often associated with adoption, in several countries a large percentage of persons seeking to adopt already have children of their own.

22. *Birth mothers who give up their children for the purpose of adoption tend to be young and unmarried.* However, having an extramarital birth, which in the past was a strong reason for placing a child for adoption, is no longer strongly associated with the availability of adoptable children. In many societies, unmarried women are deciding to raise children born out of wedlock instead of placing them for adoption.

23. *Despite the perceived shortage of adoptable children domestically, the number of children in foster care or in institutions generally far exceeds the number of children who are being adopted.* This paradox arises because many children in foster care or in institutions are older or have health problems and are not, therefore, easy to place among prospective adoptive parents who prefer younger and healthy children. In addition, because many children in foster care or in institutions still have ties to their biological parents, they often are not formally adoptable.

24. *In countries highly affected by the AIDS epidemic, there are a large number of orphans who have lost both their parents to the disease and that could be adopted either domestically [or] internationally.* It is estimated that in Africa, the continent most affected by the epidemic, the current number of domestic adoptions would have to be multiplied by 2,000 to ensure that the estimated 7.7 million orphans on the continent would have an adoptive family. At a global level, the number of adoptions would have to increase by a factor of 60 to provide families to all AIDS orphans.

Despite the perceived shortage of adoptable children domestically, the number of children in foster care or in institutions generally far exceeds the number of children who are being adopted.

---

25. *Many countries have ratified multilateral, regional or bilateral agreements on intercountry adoption aimed at addressing conflicts of jurisdiction and protecting the welfare of children.* Seventy countries have ratified or acceded to the [Hague] Convention on Protection of Children and Co-operation in Respect of Intercountry Adoption. As of January 2007, 117 countries had ratified the United Nations Optional Protocol to the Convention on the Rights of the Child on the Sale of Children, Child Prostitution and Child Pornography, which

stipulates that coercive adoption should be a criminal offence. Nevertheless, child trafficking and selling of children for adoption are still a concern in several countries. Problems in making the various agreements operational have also emerged. Initiatives are under way to ensure that existing international legal mechanisms respond better to the evolving challenges raised by intercountry adoptions.

26. *Total lack of data on adoption or limitations in the data available represent a major obstacle to the understanding of the determinants of adoption, its changing patterns over space and time, and its major trends.* Out of the 195 countries considered in this study, only 118 publish data on the total number of adoptions and far fewer publish data on adoptions classified by type (domestic vs. intercountry) or on the characteristics of those involved in the adoption process (the adopted child, the biological parents and the adoptive parents). Variations in the concepts and definitions underlying the data available limit the usefulness of cross-country comparisons.

In the United Kingdom, the Adoption Process Must Be Reformed

Rosemary Bennett and David Taylor

In the following viewpoint, London Times *reporters Rosemary Bennett and David Taylor report on the efforts of their newspaper and British prime minister David Cameron to raise awareness about the need for adoptive parents to come forward and give homes to children who are under the government's care in foster homes and institutions. They believe that governmental bureaucracy slows the process and that it must be streamlined to prevent children from languishing for years in foster care rather than being a permanent part of a loving family.*

As you read, consider the following questions:

1. According to the viewpoint, what will the Green Paper do?

2. According to David Cameron, how long on average does it take for a black child to be adopted? A white child?

3. Who is Martin Narey, as reported by the authors?

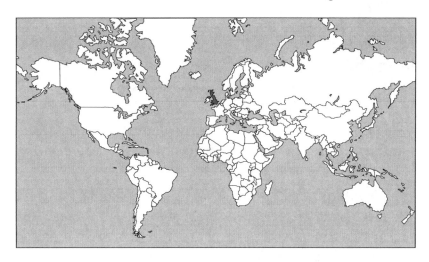

David Cameron [British prime minister] admits that it's been a challenging morning as he sinks into an armchair in his Downing Street office. "Samantha had to go off somewhere and I was in charge of the children," he says. "It was chaotic. Being a parent is bloody hard."

He has been giving a lot of thought lately to the state's duty as parent to the 65,000 children who are in the care system because they have been abused or neglected by their families.

"There is no greater responsibility than bringing up children, and no greater responsibility for the state than a child in care," he says. But he is dissatisfied with what he has found, and in particular that so few children are finding new permanent families through adoption.

The *Times'* campaign to both boost the number of adoptions—from about 3,000 a year—and speed up the adoption process has Mr Cameron's firm backing. He has now promised that a Green Paper will be published shortly, setting out new minimum standards not just for the number of adoptions but for what happens to children in the care system.

What has spurred him into action? Constituents have told him of the lengthy and bureaucratic process they have faced when trying to be approved as adoptive parents. "They don't expect it to be rushed, but I think there is a problem there," he says.

A second factor is his close friendship with Michael Gove, the education secretary, who was adopted as a baby and is passionate about the subject. Tim Loughton, the junior education minister, raised the issue frequently in opposition and in government has made it his priority.

"The third thing," Mr Cameron says, "is the figures speak volumes. There are over 60,000 children in care. I know one mustn't oversimplify things and that many of those children are travelling through care and will go back to their parents, but there were only 3,000 adoptions last year [2010], 20 per cent down on 2005 and we were not doing that well in 2005."

[British prime minister] David Cameron has been giving a lot of thought lately to the state's duty as parent to the 65,000 children who are in the care system.

Earlier Attempts at Reform

He is not the first prime minister to try to overhaul the system. [Former British prime minister] Tony Blair tried to boost the number of adoptions by setting a target for local authorities to increase the number of children adopted each year by 50 per cent. There was a cash incentive for those who managed it. The numbers went up, but he was accused of skewing the system and the targets lapsed. The numbers soon fell back again. This prime minister says that he has learnt from the mistake made by Mr Blair and his penchant for targets.

"You do have to be careful. If you select one figure, one target, councils will aim to meet that. You'll find they are doing very well on, say, having babies under one adopted but then their fostering stops working.

"I see [the new policy] as a range of 'floor standards' including the educational attainment of children in care, placement stability, proportion of children adopted from care and the timeliness of adoption."

Where councils consistently fail to meet the standards, other local authorities or charities operating in the field will be invited in to take over. That has worked well in the North London borough of Harrow, which voluntarily called in the Coram children's charity to join its adoption department. Harrow is now held up as the example for others to follow, increasing the numbers of children adopted and cutting the time it takes to place children with their new families.

Powers to strip councils of duties to run schools and children's services are already in place. What has been missing up to now is a clear indication of what failure looks like. The Green Paper will make clear what is expected in the future. Mr Cameron intends each local authority's performance to be made public in annual league tables, bringing to bear the pressure of "naming and shaming".

"We need to publish the facts and figures," he says. "I know some people don't like league tables, but I don't care. Let's publish the data and let's compare performance. It's worked in education."

The Courts Complicate Adoption

He is anxious not to appear to have a simplistic view of a complex problem, and it is not just local authorities and social workers that are in his sights. The courts are a further complication in adoption, with delays there meaning that the average time taken for a child to be adopted is two years and seven months.

The Norgrove review into family justice will be published later this week [November 2011] and Mr Cameron hopes that strong recommendations on the timing of care proceedings will be made.

"Figures for court cases are chilling," he says. "Some judges are looking for evidential standards that just don't exist. That is certainly the story I get anecdotally. The judge has a huge responsibility, but endless calls for more information and more reports to try and close off every avenue of concern mean the longer children are left in care, the worse the outcomes get. I know it is a cliché, but don't let the best be the enemy of the good.

"There is an element of judgment that is required. We've got to give people the sense of discretion and judgment, rather than thinking you can reduce to percentage zero any risk. You can't. If there is a need for legal reform beyond Norgrove, then we will do that."

The courts are a further complication in adoption, with delays there meaning that the average time taken for a child to be adopted is two years and seven months.

On the thorny issue of race, he is determined to take a stand. "Why should a black child wait 1,300 days to be adopted and a white child 900 days, when 900 days is much too long? It is one of those areas where you need to take a strong stand. You can debate and discuss all difficulties endlessly, or take a clear view that if you can get children adopted into a warm and loving home relatively rapidly, the outcomes for those children will be better.

"So let's have that as one of our goals, a clear view, and not split the difference with everyone else involved. My clear view is there isn't enough adoption, it's happening too slowly and too many children are being let down."

Adoptive Parents Will Be Recruited

Adoption reforms will be accompanied by a recruitment drive, urging the public to consider adopting or fostering. Mr Cameron realises that this may fall on deaf ears, with many pro-

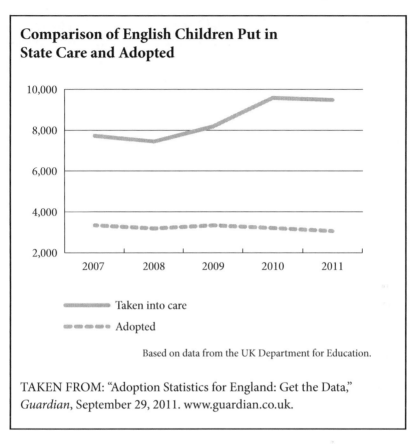

Comparison of English Children Put in State Care and Adopted

Taken into care

Adopted

Based on data from the UK Department for Education.

TAKEN FROM: "Adoption Statistics for England: Get the Data," *Guardian*, September 29, 2011. www.guardian.co.uk.

spective parents rightly saying that they have come forward before and been turned away or subjected to six months of intrusive questioning and assessing by social workers. He looks despondent. "I've heard about the three-page pet assessment. This is where we have a wider problem. It's not just in adoption. A culture of responsibility and judgment has been replaced with box-ticking and irresponsibility.

"A case came to my attention of someone who would make a brilliant parent who is adopting an Ethiopian child. It took a long time but she was happy to do it because she was so keen. The endless wait you face adopting from the care system in Britain, with no certainty that you will ever get there, is more than some people can bear, and so people are being lost to the system."

He is determined to change that. "It's not just me saying, 'Come on, British parents, come forward'. It's part of a package. We are rolling up our sleeves and doing something about it. So we are saying, 'Please come forward and we will make it different.'"

[The *Times* adoption] campaign was inspired by your anger.

The *Times* Campaigns for Adoptions

In April the *Times* began a campaign to increase the number of adoptions of children in care and streamline the process to cut delays.

The campaign was largely in response to anger among readers, who were alarmed at reports in this newspaper about the diminishing number of children being adopted, and the suspicious treatment of prospective adoptive parents by local authorities.

Readers felt particularly sorry for couples who were being rejected for adoption in England because they were white or "too middle class".

[The Times *adoption] campaign was largely in response to anger among readers, who were alarmed at reports . . . about the diminishing number of children being adopted.*

To make informed and detailed recommendations on reform of the system, the *Times* commissioned a 20,000-word report by Martin Narey, formerly the head of Barnardo's [adoption agency] and now the government's adoption adviser. While at Barnardo's, Mr Narey had expressed concern that adoption had fallen out of fashion as the best solution for children who were unable to live with the families they were born into. "The research shows that while care improves matters for children, adoption transforms their life chances and it needs to be given greater priority," he said.

His report made a series of recommendations on speeding up procedures; pursuing adoption for many more children as soon as possible when they come into the care system; and better treatment for couples who would like to adopt.

The government has accepted many of these recommendations and pledged to overhaul the system in the way Mr Narey suggested.

David Cameron wants to speed up the adoption process to encourage more prospective parents to come forward. "The endless wait you face adopting from the care system in Britain, with no certainty that you will ever get there, is more than some people can bear," he says. "We are rolling up our sleeves and doing something about it."

Lost Generation: Adoption in America Has Collapsed; Here's What to Do About It

Kevin D. Williamson

In the following viewpoint, Kevin D. Williamson argues that there are too few babies available for adoption for two reasons: First, abortion laws allow women to abort children rather than put them up for adoption; and second, transracial adoption is frowned upon by those placing children for adoption. He further argues that there ought to be market-based reform of adoption laws, allowing for the sale and purchase of parental rights. He asserts that allowing adoptive parents to contract with birth parents would provide motivation for more mothers to bear healthy children and place them for adoption. Williamson is the deputy managing editor of the National Review, *a conservative newsmagazine.*

As you read, consider the following questions:

1. Who did a 1961 *Time* magazine article profile, according to the viewpoint?

2. As reported by the author, what is the Multiethnic Placement Act of 1994, and what did it forbid?

3. According to the viewpoint, who is Richard Posner?

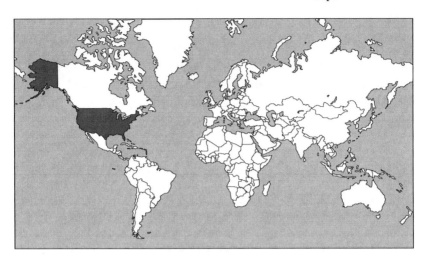

Adoption is an unexpectedly rare phenomenon in the United States, and that's a supply-side problem. The U.S. is the third most populous country in the world, and each year more than a third of our country's 4 million births are to unmarried women, but it is estimated that in a typical year the total number of mothers who voluntarily relinquish their children for adoption is fewer than 14,000—barely enough to make a statistical radar blip on the demographic Doppler. Would-be parents trek to the Far East and mount expeditions to South America because there are so few infants available for adoption in the United States.

At the same time, a half million children languish in foster care, awaiting permanent adoptive homes. There are would-be parents who want to adopt them, too, but this situation is more complex: Older children are less eagerly sought after, and the longer a child is in foster care the less likely he is to find a permanent home. The lot of these foster children has been made worse by years of bad public policy discouraging transracial adoptions—a significant barrier, since most of the couples looking to adopt are white and the children in foster care are disproportionately nonwhite. Supply and demand are wildly out of sync: If we were talking about consumer goods instead of children, we'd call this a market failure. And some of the most incisive critics of U.S. adoption policy are calling for reforms that would make adoption policies look a lot more like a market—that is, a system characterized by free and open cooperation—and a lot less like a welfare bureaucracy.

As an American institution, adoption is in decline and has been for 35 years. The decline isn't in the number of families looking to adopt; that number has remained constant for decades, around 2 percent of all married couples. The decline has come rather in the number of American women who choose to give their children up for adoption. From 1952 to 1972, one in five white unwed mothers chose adoption, according to the National Survey of Family Growth. The rates of adoption were lower for black and Hispanic women, but even so, nearly one in ten unwed mothers overall chose adoption over raising children without a husband. On January 22, 1973, the cultural earthquake that was *Roe v. Wade* changed all that. By 1981, the number of adoptions was down to 4 percent of all children born out of wedlock. The number for black children fell below 1 percent.

Roe v. Wade was of a piece with the culture of permissiveness and extended adolescence that had its roots in the postwar generation but truly bloomed in the 1970s. In these years the more radical iterations of feminism were ascendant, together with the budding homosexual-rights movement and similar expressions of the liberationist ethic of the day. Divorce rates soared as the promise of lifelong marriage, once the rock of American civil society, began its melancholy, long, withdrawing whimper. And what had been murder on Sunday night was a constitutional right by Monday morning.

Roe ushered in a culture that not only served to diminish the stigma once conjoined to premarital sex and consequent unwed motherhood, but also ensured that those babies who survived to birth were born to women who were much less likely to choose adoption. The same markers that had once identified young unmarried mothers as more likely to choose adoption—being white, relatively affluent, and relatively educated, with higher educational and career aspirations—today mark women as being likely to choose abortion. The maternity home went the way of the shotgun wedding, vanishing from the cultural landscape along with its euphemistic cousin, the months a pregnant girl spent "visiting family" prior to a quietly arranged adoption. Affluent white women tend to have fewer unwanted pregnancies across the board and, being more thoroughly secular, have been quick to avail themselves of abortion's convenience. As a consequence, the sort of child most likely to have ended up with an adoptive family a generation ago is the sort most likely to have been eliminated in one of the 50 million abortions that have occurred in the United States since 1973.

The sort of child most likely to have ended up with an adoptive family a generation ago is the sort most likely to have been eliminated in one of the 50 million abortions that have occurred in the United States since 1973.

It may be that the widespread practice of infant adoption was doomed to be a short-term phenomenon. Like so much of modern American community life, adoption was profoundly influenced by the career of Theodore Roosevelt and the reformist movements to which he lent his vitality. Prior to the 20th century, adoption of nonrelatives had been rare; orphans and children whose parents could not or would not care for them were relegated to orphanages. The Dickensian conditions at these orphanages—to say nothing of their insalubrious indoorsiness—inevitably attracted the improving passion of President Roosevelt. In 1909 he convened the first White House Conference on the Care of Dependent Children and established as a matter of national policy that, where possible, homeless children should be placed in permanent adoptive homes. A new maxim was handed down from the bully pulpit: "Home life is the highest and finest product of civilization," Roosevelt said. "Children should not be deprived of it except for urgent and compelling reasons." The idea was radical at the time and was resisted by the institutional interests attached to orphanages. But the movement was hugely successful: Within a few decades, the tribes of homeless children that had once been common sights in American cities had vanished, while the Child Welfare League of America had helped to establish standards and practices for adoption and foster parenting.

Since its early days, modern adoption has been a lightning rod for class and race anxieties. But while race, sex, and disabilities remain important considerations for many adoptive parents, Americans have grown steadily more eager to adopt children of different races. And adoptive families have been ahead of the curve: During adoption's postwar heyday, adoptive families sprinted over the color line that would not be transgressed in other areas of American life for decades. A 1961 *Time* magazine article profiled Yonkers fireman Joe Treacy and his wife, who over the course of 20 years provided foster care to more than 300 children of varying races and nationalities. When questioned by a neighbor about the provenance of two black babies he was seen parading down the sidewalk in a stroller, the fireman answered: "They're my wife's by a previous marriage." It may be a simple matter of evolutionary biology, but it's hard to be bigoted toward babies. Hard, but not impossible: As Jonah Goldberg has pointed out in these pages and elsewhere, the eugenicists at Planned Parenthood and allied organizations didn't want the children of the destitute, the black, or the sickly to be raised by adoptive families—they wanted them eliminated. After 1973 they would see their wish substantially fulfilled.

The unborn children of the post-*Roe* era are the true Lost Generation. With abortion having taken some 50 million American children out of the adoption equation, it's no surprise that would-be adoptive parents have been sent packing across the Himalayas and Andes. But what of the 500,000 or so children relegated to foster care at any given time? Unhappily, politics has conspired against them, too.

Parents' attitudes toward transracial adoption have become much more liberal since the 1970s, but the racial attitudes of social workers, those sometimes pitiless gatekeepers on the adoption pilgrimage, have hardened.

Adoption in Black and White

The phrase "out of wedlock" has a chalky, anachronistic taste, but in this context it is a necessary distinction. Married women practically never voluntarily relinquish their children for adoption. Not all adoptions are conceived in voluntary circumstances, however. Each year thousands of negligent or abusive parents, singles and married couples alike, have their parental rights terminated by the courts and their children relegated to institutional care or foster families. While some of these children are older teens who will spend only a year or two in foster homes before reaching adulthood and legal emancipation, many are young—the median age is 8.4 years—and adoption is, in most cases, the aspiration of the children's legal custodians.

For children in foster care, the calculus of adoption is complex. The older a child gets, the less likely he is to find a permanent adoptive family. Research suggests that white parents have their rights terminated earlier and more often than do black and Hispanic parents; this may give the impression that whites are being treated more harshly, but it is black and Hispanic children who are injured by this disparity. They are put on the road to adoption at a later age, placing them at a permanent disadvantage. They spend more time in foster care and are more likely to suffer from behavioral problems. All of these factors make it less likely that they will find permanent, stable homes.

Most of the parents waiting to adopt are white; most of the children awaiting adoption are not. Parents' attitudes toward transracial adoption have become much more liberal since the 1970s, but the racial attitudes of social workers, those sometimes pitiless gatekeepers on the adoption pilgrimage, have hardened. A study published by the academic journal *Child Welfare* found that 43 percent of the caseworkers responsible for the longest-waiting black children in New York State expressed hostility toward transracial adoption. Federal law prohibits the use of racial criteria in adoption placement, but ethnic considerations have seeped into the system. The number of transracial adoptions executed each year remains tiny despite the willingness of the majority of couples to adopt a child of a different race. About 8 percent of all adoptions are transracial or cross-cultural—and that number includes international adoptions, commonly from Asia and South America. Prof. Judy Fenster of Adelphi University finds that black social workers are particularly inimical to the prospect of cross-racial adoption. It seems that the matchmakers at the heart of the adoption system are part of the problem.

Transracial adoption is a volcanically touchy issue—the National Association of Black Social Workers has deployed weapons-grade rhetoric characterizing the practice as "cultural genocide." That ideology has had predictable consequences: Black children spend more time in foster care than others, and in general have less luck in finding permanent adoptive homes. The Multiethnic Placement Act of 1994, a legacy of the late senator Howard Metzenbaum, forbade the use of race as the decisive factor in making adoption-placement decisions, but the language of the statute left those politically opposed to transracial adoptions with room for much mischievous maneuvering. Would-be adoptive parents were disqualified for expressing political opinions at odds with social workers' preferences. Just as the social workers of Teddy Roosevelt's day defended the orphanages against the president's radical drive for adoptions, their professional descendants have defended racial practices that allow them to impose their own political preferences as policy.

In one case, a white couple who had hoped to adopt a severely disabled black girl in 1994 was disqualified on political grounds—specifically that they expressed a desire to raise their children to be "colorblind"—and on racial grounds, specifically that they lived in Alaska, which was judged to be superabundantly Caucasian. The couple had raised other severely disabled children of various ethnic backgrounds but they were rejected in favor of a single woman who expressed the "correct" racial attitudes—and who ended up declining to adopt the child, precisely because of her disabilities. The girl in question suffered from fetal alcohol syndrome and from Russell-Silver syndrome, a form of dwarfism associated with, among other things, gastrointestinal difficulties, a triangular face, and asymmetrical body growth. It is difficult to imagine that her most pressing challenge in life was going to be the relative scarcity of black neighbors in Fairbanks. . . .

A Market for Adoption

The fight over transracial placements is only one small intersection in the nexus between politics and adoption. There are a number of policy initiatives in the works to support adoption, from increasing the financial incentives to adopt children out of foster care to protecting the First Amendment rights of faith-based adoption agencies. One important piece of legislation is Rep. Phil English's "Religious Freedom for Providers of Adoption, Foster Care, and Child Welfare Services Act," which would prohibit punishing adoption agencies for declining to work with homosexual couples. Catholic Charities in Massachusetts suspended their adoption activities when the state attempted to force them to abandon their moral objections to facilitating adoption by homosexual couples, leaving the Bay State's children bereft of an important ally in their search for families.

Representative English, a Pennsylvania Republican, says matter-of-factly that his legislation is going nowhere: "This is the kind of legislation that this Congress is afraid to bring up for fear of offending the gay lobby," he says. And even if Pelosi and Reid weren't sitting like hens on a do-nothing Congress while hoping to hatch a more potent majority in November, the abortion lobby—the real conscience of the Democratic Party—views pro-adoption forces as a wing of the pro-life movement, rivals in a zero-sum game between the abortion ethic and the life ethic. Adoptions are as common in blue states as in red states, but adoption does not electrify Democratic leaders with the voltage of abortion or gay marriage.

Against this background, it is unsurprising that adoption supporters are not strongly focused on Washington. The National Council for Adoption has a legislative agenda, to be sure, but their most recent campaign isn't aimed at Capitol Hill; it's aimed at young mothers and fathers. Called "I Choose Adoption," it is intended to communicate that mothers who give their children to adoptive families aren't doing so because they're bad mothers, but because they are good mothers.

"We're trying to enlighten people's understanding of and appreciation for birth mothers," says NCFA president Thomas Atwood. "Adoption is a positive option, and we view birth mothers as loving, responsible parents who made a decision in the best interest of the child. The definition of a good parent is someone who does what's best for her child. She can feel right about what she's done, see herself as a good mother. Because she is."

Politicians love to dress their pet causes in swaddling clothes and declare that we have to do thus and such "for the children." But here's an issue that is literally about the children—defenseless, vulnerable children without families—and politics is hurting them. So while the NCFA is to be commended for its efforts to reach out to unwed mothers, it may be that helping unwed mothers feel good about adoption isn't enough. Why not get the politicians out of the way and stack some money on the table? To the extent that politics is the problem, the best reform may be to get politics out of adoption entirely.

It is necessary to be cautious when talking about market-based reforms of adoption practices. To American ears, that sounds like establishing a marketplace for babies, which justly sets off Klaxons of moral alarm. Under any decent system of adoption, children are people, not commodities, and people have rights that it is the duty of society to protect. It's not a question of buying and selling babies, but of freely contracting to exchange parental rights—which is, after all, what adoption is: an exchange of parental rights. And there is significant money involved in the process. What market-oriented adoption reforms are intended to accomplish is to align the incentives of unprepared parents with those of adoptive families in order to provide the best outcomes for children.

Richard Posner, a giant in the law-and-economics movement long before he became a judge on the U.S. Seventh Circuit Court of Appeals, has argued for the deregulation of the adoption system and its replacement by a market-based alternative since the publication of his paper "The Regulation of the Market in Adoptions" back in 1987. "The adoption market exhibits all of the pathologies of price regulation," Posner says. "First, there's a huge supply-demand imbalance. We have 1.5 million abortions a year but a shortage of babies available for adoption, and that suggests something is wrong. Second, there's a black market and a grey market in adoption, where doctors and lawyers act as middlemen and collect fees." The fees related to adoption can be dodgy; it's illegal to pay a fee

47

to secure a child, but there are all sorts of other fees that act as proxies for those verboten payments. The numbers coming out of grey-market adoption cases suggest would-be mothers could expect compensation of $30,000-$60,000 plus prenatal expenses—not an insignificant incentive.

Posner's efforts to account for the economic realities of adoption have been taken up and amplified by others, notable among them the economist Donald Boudreaux, who points out that there already is a market for adoption. "Parental rights are bought and sold," Boudreaux said, "but they're sold in a hidden way. If you look at the fees that adoption agencies charge, there's no itemized schedule that puts a price on parental rights. The people who do, de facto, profit from selling parental rights are the adoption agencies or adoption lawyers—the middlemen—precisely because of the artificial scarcity of the thing that they sell." Lots of money is changing hands, but little or none of it goes to the mothers who are, along with their babies, the most vulnerable parties in these transactions.

What market-oriented adoption reforms are intended to accomplish is to align the incentives of unprepared parents with those of adoptive families in order to provide the best outcomes for children.

Boudreaux defended the market-based approach with great clarity in the libertarian *Cato Journal*: "When a birth mother gives a child up for adoption, she legally transfers her parental rights to the adoptive parents; the adoptive parents gain all those rights, but only those rights, that the birth mother possessed before the adoption. Such rights are those that all non-derelict parents have in their children. The rights do not include license to abuse the child or to use him or her as a slave. . . . Branding the sale of parental rights 'baby selling' provokes people reflexively but wrongly to assume that some horror akin to slavery is being advocated." In a recent conversation with *National Review*, Boudreaux characterized the objections to the free exchange of parental rights in an open market as a question of taste: "The objections are for the most part aesthetic. It strikes people as unseemly. But they don't stop and think through the ramifications." Boudreaux argues that adoptive families would still have to be screened and the adoption approved, possibly by a judge.

Allowing adoptive parents to contract directly with mothers would, Boudreaux argues, create incentives that favor healthy babies who are well cared for and who end up in loving homes. "We allow parents who desperately want children to have them, and the mother profits from transferring her rights," Boudreaux says. "Regardless of how you feel about the morality of abortion—and I'm pro-abortion—it's hard to argue that the child is worse off. I don't see who loses out on that deal. And women have better incentives to take care of themselves prenatally—parents who contract for adoptions are not going to go into it willy-nilly, and there will be mechanisms to monitor the health of the child, so women will have an incentive not to drink or use drugs while pregnant."

Given a choice between a calcified adoption bureaucracy—one in thrall to racial ideologies and marred by the inevitable dysfunction of politics—or an imperfect but free system that helps to align economic incentives with the best interests of vulnerable women and children, the Posner-Boudreaux prescription is compelling. Economic incentives are part of every aspect of human life, and especially of family life. Many older professional couples find themselves looking to adopt because they have delayed marriage and childbirth for economic reasons. Economic calculation is probably the single biggest factor influencing how many children couples have and when they have them. Why not use economic incentives to make adoption safe, legal—and plentiful?

Teenagers Are Rarely Adopted in Canada

Justine Hunter

In the following viewpoint, Justine Hunter describes the plight of many teenagers who languish in the Canadian foster care system without much hope of adoption. She argues that governments must work harder to place these children because of the expense involved in having them in foster care and the growing shortages of foster parents. The viewpoint highlights one family who took a chance on adopting a teenager with great success. Hunter is the British Columbia politics writer for the Canadian newspaper the Globe and Mail.

As you read, consider the following questions:

1. Why are costs of foster care spiking in Canada, as reported by the author?
2. What province has done the best job in improving adoption rates, according to the viewpoint?
3. How much did British Columbia spend in 2009 on keeping children in government care, according to the viewpoint?

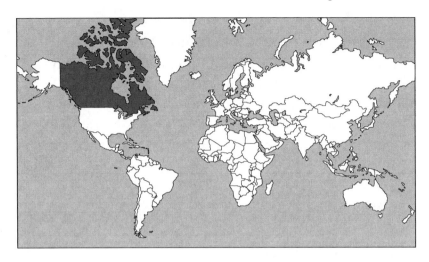

They met in a soup kitchen of a Winnipeg street mission. Wayne and Dianne Leighton were visiting their adult son who was feeding the homeless who gathered at the Vineyard Church. Dawn, just 15 years old, had run away from her foster home and was sheltering there while she figured out what she calls her "crazy headspace."

The Leightons reached out and invited Dawn to be their tour guide as they explored the city the next day. "The first day I spent with them, I thought it would be amazing to be one of their children," she said in an interview this week [July 2009].

But who adopts teenagers? The Leightons were assured the troubled youth was being placed in another foster home, and they returned to their home on Vancouver Island. But Dawn had caught a taste of something. It was her turn to reach out. One year and much complicated paperwork later, she would be a Leighton.

So rarely do Canadians think of adopting teenagers, the family's application to adopt Dawn must have stood out like a red flag.

But as governments struggle with the poor outcomes and rising costs of keeping children in care, it's surprising there isn't more effort to find permanent homes for the thousands of kids who are not going back to their birth parents.

Even before the B.C. [British Columbia] government's latest frenzy of cost-containment exercises, officials in the Ministry of Children and Family Development were fretting about the expense of maintaining kids in care. Last summer, an internal report pointed to a 24 per cent increase in its cost for maintaining a child or youth in a foster home—money that isn't improving the level of care they receive.

Costs are spiking because kids in care have increasingly complex needs and there is a growing shortage of skilled foster parents. The result: Foster parents are routinely pushed to take on more than they are qualified for and the gaps are filled with more costly "last resort" group homes and other contracted services with lower standards of care.

As governments struggle with the poor outcomes and rising costs of keeping children in care, it's surprising there isn't more effort to find permanent homes for . . . thousands of kids.

An Overburdened System

It's an overburdened system waiting for the next breakdown.

Most of the kids in the system today are lifers—kids growing up in government care with little hope of finding a permanent family. When they turn 19, they are on their own.

"There are a whole bunch of people who don't accept the adoptability of older kids," noted Maris Blechner. Her adoption agency in Little Neck, N.Y., specializes in teens and special-needs children. She regularly travels to Canada to spread the word about how to change the bias against uniting kids like Dawn with families like the Leightons.

"Is everyone working as hard as they can to find a family for these kids?" she challenges. Ms. Blechner is part of a movement in the U.S. to encourage adoption by someone already in the child's world—a grandparent, a therapist, a coach. "If these kids can't go home, let's look at who else in the child's life could adopt them."

Mary Polak is B.C.'s newest minister to the revolving door that is the Ministry of Children and Family Development. Sure, she said, adoption is great: "Obviously a forever home is the best circumstance for any of those kids, so we're always looking for ways of how we can advance how popular adoption is."

But Sandra Scarth, president of the Adoption Council of Canada, said B.C.'s support has waxed and waned as the Children's Ministry repeatedly changes ministers, changes deputies, changes direction—it's not a recipe for the sustained recruitment programs needed to improve adoption rates. "If you want a province that has done the best job consistently, it's Alberta," she said. Stability for kids, when the government is the parent, starts at the top.

So who would want to adopt an older child? Older child-less couples, empty nesters—people who want to expand their family but are daunted by the notion of diapers and toddler tantrums.

Cheryl Fix is executive director of the Victoria-based CHOICES Adoption & Counselling, which has negotiated access to government lists of children in care who are available for adoption. She spends a lot of effort "marketing" the idea of adoption for older kids.

"It's a fairly new concept in Canada," she said. Many caseworkers don't think of pushing for adoption—it generally takes longer with older kids because the child too must be involved in the decision making.

So who would want to adopt an older child?

Older childless couples, empty nesters—people who want to expand their family but are daunted by the notion of diapers and toddler tantrums. The agency just placed three teenaged brothers with a single dad who has worked in group homes and was comfortable with the teen dynamic.

The payback? Knowing you're the one they can come home to at Christmas, being the one to walk them down the aisle one day in the not-so-distant future.

Wayne Leighton said the unplanned expansion of the family has been rewarding but it is also a "convoluted, uphill journey" as his youngest learns to fly after a lifetime of not trusting that someone will be there to catch her. . . .

There are no firm statistics for the number of teens across Canada who are available for adoption, but the B.C. government does track the children in its care who are seeking a permanent home.

- Families interested in adopting a teen: 29

- Teens in care who would like to be adopted: 386

- Teens in care who were adopted last year: 17

- Largest segment of children in care, by age: 14–16

B.C. will spend $230 million this year on keeping kids in government care, an average of $31,170 for each child. Costs are rising because demand is growing and the supply of caregivers is shrinking. Here are some reasons why, according to an internal government report in July 2008.

The Needs Are Greater

The needs of children in care are becoming more severe. Staff reported "nine-year-olds who need 24-hour, double staffing in residential facilities, five- and seven-year-olds who have been excluded from school, and 13-year-olds dealing with drug addiction and pregnancy."

Staff also warned that children in care are having difficulty accessing services for various developmental disabilities and mental-health issues. "These unmet needs may be increasing the severity of behaviours among the children in care population."

Fewer Caregivers

Skilled foster parents are aging, juggling high housing costs and increased demands from the government. Increasingly they are lured away by higher-paying work or converting to serve more lucrative and less stressful foreign-exchange students.

Group homes are struggling to recruit and retain staff as well: One participant at a recruitment session "questioned why someone would want to work in a group home with violent youth for $12/hour when they could work down the street at Tim Hortons [restaurant] for $16/hour."

Adoption Is Well Accepted in Uganda

Moses Talemwa and Abu-Baker Mulumba

In the following viewpoint, Moses Talemwa and Abu-Baker Mulumba suggest that celebrities such as Madonna could adopt a baby in Uganda more easily than in Malawi. Despite the support for adoption, however, the process is nonetheless tedious and time consuming. Many adoptions in Uganda occur informally, when a local guardian adopts a child from an orphanage without having to go to court. The viewpoint concludes with the story of a successful gospel singer who was adopted at a young age. Talemwa and Mulumba are journalists who write for the Ugandan Observer.

As you read, consider the following questions:

1. In Uganda, where does the adoption process usually start, according to the viewpoint?
2. About how many children were adopted in 2008, according to the viewpoint?
3. As reported by the authors, how was Wilson Bugembe orphaned?

U S singer Madonna could have avoided all the trouble she went through while adopting a child from Malawi, if she

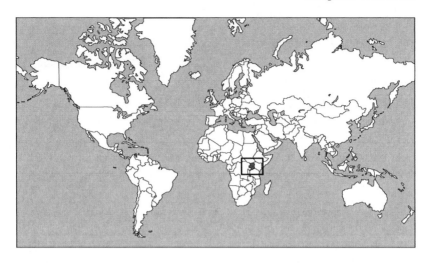

had sought a Ugandan child instead. That is the verdict of High Court Deputy Registrar, Family Division, Batema Ndika-bona.

The registrar confirms that indeed more foreign nationals are adopting Ugandan children and the hurdles in the adoption process are not as pronounced as in Malawi. . . .

Batema's conclusion follows a case in which a Canadian consular officer, Darryl Hyard, travelled from his office in Nairobi to inquire about the growing number of Ugandan children whose guardians were turning up in his office to seek visas to Canada.

The Canadian official was concerned that children as young as two years were being offered for adoption even though the law provides for legal guardianship after the child has had two years of bonding with the intending parent. However, the registrar says the court reserves the right to grant a parent legal guardianship at any time.

The Process of Adopting a Ugandan Child

Regardless of that, the process of adopting a child is quite tedious. The process usually starts with a visit to a certified orphanage where one selects a child. After selection, a social worker from the orphanage visits the home of the adopting parent to make a report on whether the parent is suitable.

A probation officer in the division is also supposed to make an independent report on the candidate parent's suitability. Those reports are given to the candidate parent, who attaches them to a formal letter to the High Court Registrar in charge of the Family Division seeking permission to foster a child.

Fostering a child refers to bonding with the child for three years before the court can determine that the parent is suitable. In the meantime, the parent posts a photograph of the child in the papers to ensure the registrar forwards the matter to the judge who holds a hearing and decides on the matter.

The process of adopting a child [from Uganda] is quite tedious.

The adoption process remains with many loopholes, though. According to the registrar, there is no government department to represent the child's interests in court.

Batema says the probation officers and social workers, as well as the education or youth ministry, should present reports to the state attorney who would then advise the court on how to proceed, but this never happens. Instead, those reports are handed to the candidate parent, who is also an interested party in the matter.

In addition, the High Court can only rely on affidavits from the probation officers to determine whether the parent will be suitable for the child. Thus, it is impossible for the court to determine independently that the candidate parents will turn out to be harmful. However, Batema says the High Court attempts to rule in the best interests of the child.

Most non-Ugandan nationals who receive legal guardianship for Ugandan children are supposed to register them at Ugandan embassies abroad, but there is no follow-up to en-

---

Uganda's Orphans

Although Uganda has the second-highest birthrate in the world, many children born in this troubled nation either die young or lose their parents early. As of 2007, Uganda had an estimated 2.5 million orphans under 17 years old. Of that number, about half were orphaned by AIDS. The burden of care for these children often falls on grandparents. . . . Increasingly, dying parents or relatives unable to provide care are relinquishing infants to Uganda's orphanages.

"Our Work in Uganda,"
Holt International, 2011.
www.holtinternational.org.

---

sure that these children are well settled in. About 65 children were given out last year [2008], compared to just over half of that in 2007.

Indigenous Adoptions

But not all children are adopted in court. In fact, more children are handed over to indigenous guardians without having to go to court. Court officials say most churches in the country run children's homes, where orphans and other abandoned children are raised until a guardian can be found to look after them.

Some indigenous families will pick children from these homes and raise them as their own. In many cases these adoptive parents do not want the children to know that they were adopted. However, a few stand out. Now an accomplished singer, Pastor Wilson Bugembe was picked up by a Christian, who took the young boy to church one Sunday, where one [Stephen] Mbogo took him on.

However, Mbogo, who was also the director of Highway College, died shortly after adopting the young Bugembe along with his brother Brian. But Mbogo's wife, Maureen, decided to keep the boys along with many other children.

Bugembe has since given back to society and now lives in Nansana with a large family of teenagers, infants and others that he has adopted, including some who completed their studies at Highway College but have nowhere to go.

Some adoptive parents say they are not interested in going to court, but do it (adopt children) out of their love of God. "I do it so that the glory of God can shine through," Pastor Bugembe says.

Wilson Bugembe's Experience

Pastor Wilson Bugembe, 25, attributes his success in life to the fact that he was adopted at a very young age, and that his adoptive parents were good to him. Bugembe, a former street boy orphaned by AIDS, was adopted by Stephen (RIP) and Maureen Mbogo. The couple treated him even better than their biological children, he says.

"You never know, maybe life would have been different if I had grown up with my biological parents, but since I did not see much of them, I am very sure that Maureen has a very big place in heaven for her role in bringing me up," Bugembe says. According to the pastor, the Mbogo family loved him beyond measure and "did not look at me as a failure but they moulded me for the future."

Bugembe, together with Wilfred Rugumba and Ben Kibumba, now run an orphanage, Mercy Childcare Home. Located in Namusera, Wakiso District, Mercy Childcare Home has over 80 children. And Bugembe has to see to it that they live a better life and are trained for the future. "I'm just the head of the home but there are so many people helping me run it and those who give us offers.

"I like seeing young boys and girls live a promising life, that is why I like Ms [Rita] Nkemba whose Dwelling Places caters for more than 1,000 children," says Bugembe. The pastor says more people should be encouraged to care for and adopt disadvantaged children.

[Pastor Wilson] Bugembe, now a celebrated gospel artist, believes that if a child who has been suffering is adopted and given better opportunities, they end up working harder and aiming higher all the time.

Bugembe, now a celebrated gospel artist, believes that if a child who has been suffering is adopted and given better opportunities, they end up working harder and aiming higher all the time. "Because God makes you go through difficult times, you work very hard to change the world," he says.

Bugembe, also a senior pastor of Light the World Church, however, wishes that people who adopt children try to let them keep some of their ancestral traits. "I hope government puts a law in place to bar people who adopt children from trying to change their identity," he said.

Adoption Is Not Well Accepted in Japan

Isabel Reynolds

In the following viewpoint, Isabel Reynolds reports on the so-called "baby hatch," a device at a Japanese hospital wherein a mother can deposit her baby anonymously to put the child up for adoption. The baby hatch saves the mother public embarrassment. Some criticize the scheme because they believe it will allow parents to escape their responsibilities. Supporters, however, believe that adoption is a better outcome for children than being raised in an orphanage. Reynolds comments on the generally negative attitude Japanese people hold toward adoption. Reynolds is a Reuters reporter working in Japan.

As you read, consider the following questions:

1. About how many children are in Japan's children's homes, according to the viewpoint?

2. What is the stand of Prime Minister Shinzo Abe concerning adoption, as reported by the author?

3. According to the viewpoint, why are children's homes partly to blame for the low adoption rates in Japan?

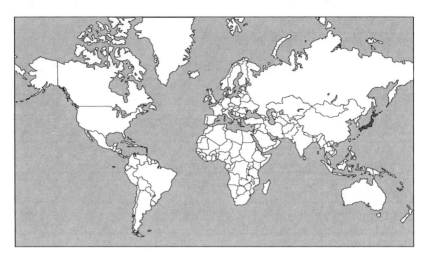

When a newborn baby girl was left in Japan's controversial "baby hatch" last week [July 2007], the child's life may have been saved, but her chances of finding new parents were slim due to a cultural aversion to adoption in Japan.

The baby is one of four tots—one of them three years old—so far left at the "stork's cradle" baby hatch at the Catholic-run Jikei Hospital in Kumamoto, southern Japan.

A small door in the outside wall of the hospital opens to reveal a tiny bed inside, allowing parents to leave their child safely and anonymously. Once they do, an alarm goes off to alert hospital staff to the new arrival.

Similar facilities exist in Germany, where babies are offered for adoption after an eight-week period during which birth parents can change their minds.

Critics of the "Baby Hatch"

But the many vocal critics of the first "baby hatch" in Japan are afraid it may encourage parents to opt out of their responsibilities. And legal barriers and prejudice against adoption in Japan may mean that children abandoned in the "baby hatch" will be raised in institutions rather than by adopted parents.

"There is a feeling that it is somehow natural for children who can't live with their parents to be in an institution," said Masaki Takakura, a journalist and author of a book on adoption.

"This is a hangover from the postwar years, when children whose parents had died were rounded up and sent to orphanages."

Legal barriers and prejudice against adoption in Japan may mean that children abandoned in the "baby hatch" will be raised in institutions rather than by adopted parents.

Local officials will not comment on specific cases, but if Japanese courts do not define the "baby hatch" children as officially "abandoned," they may be left in children's homes for years, theoretically awaiting the return of their birth parents.

The vast majority of the 30,000 children in Japan's children's homes—which are struggling to cope with increasing numbers of abused youngsters—will stay put until they are old enough to work.

Research shows growing up in an institution often leads to disadvantages in emotional development as well as education and employment, which is why many say attitudes toward adoption need to be changed in Japan.

"I used to have a very negative image of adoption and I think a lot of other people do too," explained 38-year-old housewife Tomoyo Suzuki, adding that her thinking changed after she went to a seminar about it. She and her husband went on to adopt two babies now aged three and one.

"I think a lot of people are concerned about blood ties."

Prime Minister Shinzo Abe—who criticised the "baby hatch" for encouraging parents to opt out of their responsibilities—and his wife, Akie, themselves rejected the idea of adopting.

Adopted Children Are Unusual in Japan

Ochanomizu University's [Yasuhiko] Yuzawa, who has long studied Japan's family system, says that adoptions were common practice up until around World War II for maintaining families and family businesses. The shift away from a society tolerant of adopted children occurred during Japan's postwar economic growth period.

"As less emphasis was placed on the traditional Japanese family system, adopted children came to be viewed as unusual," Yuzawa says. "An atmosphere developed in which they were subjected to prejudice, and kept secret."

"Japan: 90 Percent of 'Children in Care' Live in Institutions," Asahi Shimbun *(Osaka), November 27, 2011. ajw.asahi.com.*

Japan's Confucian Roots Discourage Adoption

Last year, Akie went public with her fertility problems and said her husband had suggested they adopt.

"I could not accept this and was not confident about bringing up an adoptee properly, so it did not happen," she told a Japanese magazine.

Those who do adopt often move house immediately afterwards to cover up their child's origins, said Kazuko Yokota of Motherly Network, a volunteer group that supports women coping with unexpected pregnancies and arranges adoptions.

Attitudes are shaped by everything from Confucian teachings to a detailed household registry system that can dog unwed mothers for their entire lives, even if they give their child up for adoption.

Confucianism, which spread to Japan from China and Korea more than a thousand years ago, emphasizes the importance of a child's relationships with its birth parents and reverence for ancestry.

"Children in need of adoption have been stigmatized by notions of pure and impure or good and bad blood," Peter Hayes of Britain's Sunderland University and Toshie Habu wrote in their book *Adoption in Japan*.

Most Adoptions Occur Within the Extended Family

For much of Japan's history, adoption has therefore remained within the extended family, with childless couples often taking in a nephew or other relative to carry on their family name or business, rather than because the child was in need of care.

"Special adoption" of needy nonrelatives was not introduced until 1989 and only a few hundred cases are approved each year, compared with three to four thousand in the United Kingdom, which has around half Japan's population.

The difference lies not only in the shortage of willing parents, but also the small number of available babies, many say.

> *For much of Japan's history, adoption has . . . remained within the extended family, with childless couples often taking in a nephew or other relative to carry on their family name or business.*

When women give birth they must enter the child's name on their family register, a powerful incentive for single women to end a pregnancy or even abandon a newborn rather than risk its being discovered by a potential employer or future husband.

"We have campaigned at least for minors to be able to leave this information off their registers, but we have been told it won't happen," said Yokota of Motherly Network.

Children's homes, which are subsidized by the government according to the number of children in their care, are partly to blame because they are reluctant to recommend candidates for adoption, says sociologist Roger Goodman of Oxford University.

"We need to spread the message that adoption is an important tool for helping children. How do we do this, given that there is no background of Christian values here?" said author Takakura.

Shocked by the fact that some adoption agencies charge huge fees to introduce Japanese babies to adoptive families abroad, he is working with sympathetic members of Parliament to try to pass a law encouraging more Japanese to take in unwanted children.

Periodical Bibliography

The following articles have been selected to supplement the diverse views presented in this chapter.

Beverly Adgraft	"A Tale of Two Cities," *Sunday Telegraph Magazine* (London), April 22, 2012.
Rosemary Bennett	"New Laws Will Speed Adoption to Give Children Greater Stability," *Times* (London), March 9, 2012.
Niki Chesworth	"Every Child Deserves a Family Life," *Evening Standard* (London), October 31, 2011.
Concord Times (Freetown, Sierra Leone)	"Sierra Leone: Adoption Protects the Child from Child Trafficking," July 11, 2011.
Shanti Gunaratnam and Sonia Ramachandran	"Baby Buying Boom," *New Straits Times* (Malaysia), February 7, 2010.
Martin Narey	"The Narey Report: Chapter 3: What's Happened to Adoption Recently," *Times* (London), July 5, 2011.
Joanna Sugden	"Hostility to Adoption Is 'Letting Children Down,'" *Times* (London), August 30, 2011.
Janice Tai	"Adoptions in Singapore Fall by Half over Last Decade; Stringent Checks, Tighter Supply, More Turning to IVF Among Reasons," *Singapore Times*, August 22, 2011.
Cheryl Wetzstein	"Increase in Adoptions Spells Fewer Children on Rolls, Shorter Waits; Advocates Cite 'Real Success' in Data," *Washington Times*, May 10, 2011.

CHAPTER 2

| Transnational Adoption

Transnational Adoptions Should Be Strictly Regulated

Kate Hilpern

In the following viewpoint, British journalist Kate Hilpern reports on an American adoptive mother's decision to return a seven-year-old adopted child to Russia alone because she no longer wanted to parent him. Hilpern considers the ethics and regulations of international adoptions and argues that such adoptions must be carefully regulated and supervised to protect children. In addition, she accuses the United States of having lax adoption rules, leading to the tragic situation of the Russian child. Hilpern writes for the British newspaper the Independent.

As you read, consider the following questions:

1. What was the name of the Russian child adopted from an orphanage by Torry-Ann Hansen, as reported by the author?

2. About how many children are adopted from overseas in the United Kingdom, according to Hilpern?

3. Why did Britain and the United States cut red tape to facilitate the adoption of children from Haiti, according to the author?

An American mother's decision to send her seven-year-old adopted son back to Russia, alone and with a note that she no longer wanted him, has horrified officials and adoption experts in both countries and made headline news worldwide. The treatment of the Russian boy, Artyom Savelyev, has been described as a "monstrous deed" by the Russian president, Dmitry Medvedev.

An International Adoption Gone Wrong

Artyom Savelyev was adopted from an orphanage last year by Torry-Ann Hansen of Tennessee. On Thursday [in April 2010], the single mother put him unaccompanied on a 10-hour flight to Moscow with a note stating: "I no longer wish to parent this child." The note is said to explain: "He is violent and has severe psychopathic issues/behaviour. I was lied to and misled by the Russian orphanage workers and director regarding his mental stability. They chose to grossly misrepresent those problems in order to get him out of their orphanage."

The Hansen family claims Artyom drew a picture of their house burning down and told [them] that he was going to burn it down with them in it. It is reported that his mother packed the boy's rucksack and told him he was going on an "excursion". Officials in the former Soviet Union deny these allegations, claiming Artyom had no mental health problems and the Russian media reported Hansen as having "cynically returned the child to Russia as if he was an unwanted purchase". Russia has since announced a freeze on child adoptions by US families.

In an interview with ABC News, the Russian president said he had a "special concern" about the recent treatment of Russian children adopted by Americans. Peter Selman, author of *Intercountry Adoption: Development, Trends and Perspectives* and visiting fellow at the School of Geography, Politics and Sociology at Newcastle University, confirms that cases range from "an American man who adopted a five-year-old Russian girl and abused her for 10 years right through to several cases of murder". International adoptions between other countries, however, don't seem to tell such sinister tales. In fact, research shows no evidence that international adoptions are any more likely to break down than domestic placements. One study of 165 children adopted from Romania found only two break-downs and other research shows that most children adopted from overseas do well in terms of developmental outcomes.

Lax Rules Govern Adoptions in the United States

Worryingly lax [rules govern adoptions] in the US, where overseas adoptions—which form the bulk of adoptions—tend to be private and there are some notoriously unethical agencies which take large sums of money. There seems to be little protection in place for children themselves. Sheriff Randall Boyce even told ABC News that there may be no crime at all on the part of Hansen—merely "some bad judgement on the way she turned this child back".

The older the child at placement, the more likely the chance of the placement failing.

Strict Adoption Rules in the United Kingdom

Here [in the United Kingdom (UK)], the number of children adopted from overseas is relatively small—around 325 a year, less than 10 per cent of all adoptions—largely because rules are so strict. The figure would almost certainly be higher, had the process not been tightened up following the notorious case of the Kilshaws in 2000—who paid to adopt twin sisters from abroad over the Internet. The system was then changed so that anyone wishing to adopt from overseas must be as-sessed by a social worker in the UK, just as they would if applying to adopt domestically. The next step is to seek permission from the British government to apply to the country in question. That country has to have signed up to the Hague Convention [on Protection of Children and Co-operation in Respect of Intercountry Adoption], which aims to ensure that in every adoption there is proof that adoption is genuinely in the best interests of the child.

The British Association for Adoption and Fostering (BAAF) estimates that one in five adoptions breaks down. The older the child at placement, the more likely the chance of the placement failing. A major study by the Maudsley Hospital also shows that adoption breakdowns tend to happen longer after the child joins the family than in this case. These researchers found a disruption rate of 8 per cent after one year and 29 per cent six years later.

"Often when you adopt a child from overseas, you will have very little background information," says a spokesman from BAAF. "The child may know nothing about his or her family of origin, which may pose significant issues for them as they get older, and medical reports for some countries may not reflect the true state of the child's health." As reports of orphanages abroad show, these children may also have suffered a particularly worrying form of neglect.

Ethical Concerns

Although the Hague convention attempts to stop child trafficking, some argue that what now happens is "child laundering"—that is, using the formal system to cover less than ideal circumstances. [American pop singer] Madonna has been heavily criticised for adopting two children from Africa as "orphans" when they have fathers.

Catriona Aldridge, who adopted three street children from Guatemala, was motivated by giving them a better life, but she's not so sure "rescuing" children, and bringing them thousands of miles from their roots, is always the answer. "It's not

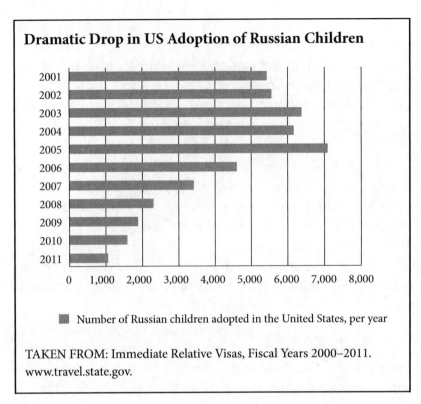

Dramatic Drop in US Adoption of Russian Children

Number of Russian children adopted in the United States, per year

TAKEN FROM: Immediate Relative Visas, Fiscal Years 2000–2011.
www.travel.state.gov.

that I'm anti-adoption or that I regret adopting. But I believe more and more that we need to improve the situation for people—for women in particular—in these developing countries," she says.

The most prominent recent controversy surrounding international adoption is Haiti. Britain and the US cut red tape in order to facilitate adoption of the hundreds of children who were believed to have been orphaned by the January [2010] earthquake. Many argue that rushing the process could jeopardise family reunification and to date, the situation remains unresolved.

The Largest Provider Countries

Most children adopted overseas come from China and Russia, but the numbers coming from China are dropping dramatically. Cynics say this is because the country recognises that this image doesn't look good and it doesn't like the idea of same-sex couples or single people adopting their children. Optimists say it's because they are starting to sort out their own problems. Either way, it is a reflection of how the countries people adopt from are constantly evolving. Some years back, the top countries were Guatemala and Romania. Not surprisingly, countries topping the list are often blighted by war or have faced natural disasters, or have had publicity surrounding the number of children in orphanages.

> *Countries topping the list [as sources of adoptees] are often blighted by war or have faced natural disasters, or have had publicity surrounding the number of children in orphanages.*

Is the System Flawed?

In the US, it's hard to see another answer than yes. And even though the UK doesn't have the poor reputation that the US does, few would argue that our system is perfect. Countries including Denmark, where overseas adoption is far more common, criticises us for using social workers with very little expertise in the issues. Others argue that we need a central government agency dedicated to international adoption.

Is International Adoption Failing the Children It Should Be Helping?

Yes . . .

- Those adopted from overseas often point to being afflicted by two key issues—loss and racism

- Adopters often go overseas because rules at home make adoption difficult—a misguided starting point

- Without proper resources from governments, how can it ever be in children's best interests?

No ...

- Children adopted from overseas are often saved from lives of misery and suffering

- Adopters often help their children to trace, find and maintain links with birth families

- There are many studies on international adoption, helping people to learn from past mistakes

New Irish Laws Change Regulations for Transnational Adoptions

Jamie Smyth

In the following viewpoint, Jamie Smyth reports on changes in Irish law concerning transnational adoptions. With the Irish ratification of the Hague convention on intercountry adoption, Irish couples find that some countries such as Vietnam are no longer eligible to send children to Ireland. A number of parents close to completing the adoption process have found that their applications are in limbo. Smyth recounts the story of one Irish couple who has waited more than five years to adopt a child from Vietnam. Smyth is the social affairs correspondent for the Irish Times.

As you read, consider the following questions:

1. As reported by the author, from how many countries can Irish couples adopt now that the Hague convention has been ratified by the Irish government?

2. How old was Nora Butler when she and her husband started the adoption process, according to the viewpoint?

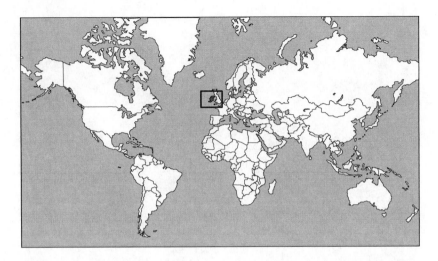

3. According to the viewpoint, about how much does it cost, in Euros, to adopt a Vietnamese child in Ireland?

The government [of Ireland] has moved to ease the concerns of people in the process of adopting children from abroad, promising a new adoption regime will provide more partner countries for them to adopt from.

It has also been claimed that the long and stressful assessment process that couples must undergo before they are allowed to adopt children should also speed up under the new regime due to begin on Monday [November 1, 2010].

Minister for Children and Youth Affairs Barry Andrews said yesterday the Adoption Act 2010, which enters into force on Monday, would open the doors to a host of new countries for Irish couples hoping to adopt abroad.

The Hague Convention Is Ratified

By ratifying the Hague Convention on [Protection of Children and Co-operation in Respect of Intercountry Adoption], Irish couples could theoretically adopt from 83 countries such as Britain, Mexico and the Philippines, he said.

The Hague convention safeguards the fundamental rights of children in intercountry adoptions, in both their country of birth and the country of adoption. Further safeguards aim to prevent the abduction, sale and trafficking of children for adoption.

Many couples going through the assessment process with the Health Service Executive [HSE] are concerned because the [Adoption] Authority [of Ireland] will not authorise new Russian adoptions because it has not ratified the Hague convention.

Russia currently supplies the largest number of adopted children to Irish couples. In 2008, 117 Irish couples adopted a child from Russia and 1,229 have been adopted from Russia since 1991.

> The Hague convention safeguards the fundamental rights of children in intercountry adoptions, in both their country of birth and the country of adoption.

Several parents of adopted children from Russia, or who are going through the adoption assessment process, told the *Irish Times* they fear there could be long delays to new countries coming on stream under the new adoption regime.

"I fear that people who get declarations to adopt after November 1st will face delays as the new adoption system beds down. The structures may take a few years to get into place," said one parent.

Mr Andrews said the Adoption Board had worked very hard to issue declarations of eligibility and suitability to adopt to ensure very few people would get caught out in the transition period.

Any couple who is provided with a declaration from the board is still allowed to proceed with an adoption from non-Hague compliant countries such as Russia for a maximum period of three years.

Mr Andrews said the new adoption authority, which will be appointed on Monday, would also move very quickly to

The Preamble to the 1993 Hague Adoption Convention

The States signatory to the present Convention,

Recognising that the child, for the full and harmonious development of his or her personality, should grow up in a family environment, in an atmosphere of happiness, love and understanding,

Recalling that each State should take, as a matter of priority, appropriate measures to enable the child to remain in the care of his or her family of origin,

Recognising that intercountry adoption may offer the advantage of a permanent family to a child for whom a suitable family cannot be found in his or her State of origin,

Convinced of the necessity to take measures to ensure that intercountry adoptions are made in the best interests of the child and with respect for his or her fundamental rights, and to prevent the abduction, the sale of, or traffic in children,

Desiring to establish common provisions to this effect, taking into account the principles set forth in international instruments, in particular the United Nations Convention on the Rights of the Child, of 20 November 1989, and the United Nations Declaration on Social and Legal Principles relating to the Protection and Welfare of Children, with Special Reference to Foster Placement and Adoption Nationally and Internationally (General Assembly Resolution 41/85, of 3 December 1986),

Have agreed upon the following provisions.

"The Hague Convention on Protection of Children and
Co-Operation in Respect of Intercountry Adoption,"
Hague Conference on Private International Law, May 29, 1993.
www.hcch.net.

agree the necessary administrative agreements with Hague compliant states to facilitate adoptions for couples.

These administrative agreements are different from the type of bilateral agreements we have negotiated between countries to facilitate adoptions. They are far less complex, said Mr Andrews.

He said he was also willing to travel to Moscow to try to agree a new bilateral adoption agreement with Russia.

Mr Andrews said the act provided for the appointment of accredited agencies to do assessments that were previously undertaken by the HSE. This would speed things up for couples, although it would take awhile for the transfer to take place, he said.

Mr Andrews said he acknowledged the pain that the closure of certain countries (Vietnam, Guatemala and Ethiopia) to Irish couples seeking to adopt abroad had caused in the past. He said he was trying to resolve the situation for 20 couples seeking adoptions in Vietnam when all adoptions to Ireland were halted in June 2009.

The Adoption Board will be formally dissolved on Monday and replaced with a new adoption authority. Child law expert Geoffrey Shannon will remain on as chairman of the authority. The authority will see the appointment of a psychologist, a social worker and a GR [doctor] to its board as decreed under the Adoption Act.

An Irish Couple Tells Their Story

Pat and Nora Butler have been trying to adopt a child from Vietnam for the past 5 1/2 years. A decision by the government to suspend adoptions from Vietnam last year has left them, and 19 other Irish couples, stuck in limbo. Here Nora tells their story:

"I was 38 years old when we started on the adoption process with the authorities. I am 42 years old now, but I still have no family," says Nora Butler.

"It is the length of time that it is taking that is the biggest problem, and your age does catch up with you. Our lives have been on hold during this whole stressful adoption process. We kept putting holidays off, thinking that we'd be travelling to Vietnam to pick up our baby. But it just hasn't happened.

A decision by the government to suspend adoptions from Vietnam last year has left [Pat and Nora Butler], and 19 other Irish couples, stuck in limbo.

"We had an unhappy experience with several IVF [in vitro fertilisation] programmes, which turned out to be unsuccessful. This took five years, so all-in-all we've been trying to start a family for a decade. Time is our biggest enemy, because the likelihood of being allowed to adopt a second child reduces as you get older.

"It took about two years before the process properly began after our application. Our social worker started our assessment and we took our pre-adoption course.

"The country that you choose to adopt from is a very personal issue for each couple. We undertook research and chose Vietnam because we thought it would be safer, as the guidelines were well established.

"Adopting from Vietnam costs about EUR 7,000, while other countries can be much more expensive than that.

"We got our declarations of eligibility and suitability to adopt after about three years. We then went to Helping Hands Adoption Mediation Agency, which mediates with the Vietnamese government.

"However, the bilateral agreement between Ireland and Vietnam lapsed in June 2009. A few months later, a report came out on Vietnamese adoptions, which was negative towards adoptions from abroad.

"About 79 Irish couples already had referrals of Vietnamese children and they were able to proceed with the adoptions.

"But 20 couples who were still awaiting referrals of children, including us, were not allowed by the government to proceed due to the findings of the report.

"We are just waiting now. The Minister for Children has told us he is trying to get the adoptions through and is awaiting a response from the Vietnamese government.

"Our biggest problem is the lack of communication from the government. We know a lot of people who are finding it very difficult to keep going. It is a very personal issue for the couples involved. We know there isn't a hope in hell of our adoption going forward this year, but I think next year it will come through for us. Vietnam is going to ratify the Hague convention next year, so we are hopeful.

"Our hearts are set on Vietnam now. If we had switched country we may have had a child by now but we see a good happy culture and a good attitude to Irish people adopting from the country."

"Baby Factories" in Nigeria Engage in Child Trafficking

Ojoma Akor

In the following viewpoint, Ojoma Akor reports on so-called "baby factories" in Nigeria. She describes situations in which pregnant teenagers visiting clinics for prenatal care are forced to give up their babies to the doctor running the clinic, who in turn sells the babies. In other situations, a woman called an "alhaja" finds pregnant women, offers to care for them during the pregnancy and delivery, and then requires their babies in payment. The babies are sold for overseas adoption, black magic rituals, prostitution, or servitude. Akor is a journalist who writes for the Nigerian newspaper the Daily Trust.

As you read, consider the following questions:

1. How much money have girls been offered for their babies, according to the viewpoint?

2. According to the author, what excuses do some pregnant teen girls give for selling their babies?

3. What does the author believe the government of Nigeria should do about the situation?

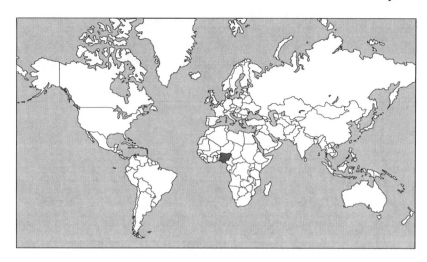

When pain and sickness made me cry who gazed upon my heavy eye and wept for fear that I should die ... my mother. This is one of the lines of a popular nursery rhyme portraying the infinite love and bond between mother and child such that some mothers are willing to give up their lives for their children in trouble or disaster situations, but with the growing trend these days of mothers willfully selling their children to buyers whose intent are glaringly sinister one wonders what has become of their maternal love and instinct.

The Police Raid a "Baby Factory"

The print and broadcast media and much of cyberspace last month [June 2011] were awash with the story of the police raid of a suspected baby factory in Aba, Abia State [Nigeria], where 32 pregnant teenage girls, who were reportedly forced to have babies in a baby-selling business under the watch of Dr. Hyacinth Orikara of the Cross Foundation Heda Clinic, were arrested along with him. These babies were allegedly offered for sale for ritual, trafficking and other purposes.

According to Abia State Police Commissioner, Bala Hassan, the police stormed the premises of the Cross Foundation in Aba following a tip-off that pregnant girls aged between 15 and 17 are being made to make babies for the proprietor.

He said, "We rescued 32 pregnant girls and arrested the proprietor who is undergoing interrogation over allegations that he normally sells the babies to people who may use them for rituals or other purposes."

Teenagers with unplanned pregnancies are sometimes lured to clinics and then forced to hand over their babies.

Some of the girls told police they had been offered to sell their babies for between 25,000 and 30,000 naira [about $160 to $220 USD] depending on the sex of the baby.

The National Agency for the Prohibition of Trafficking in Persons [and Other Related Matters] (NAPTIP) said the babies would then be sold to buyers for anything from 300,000 naira to one million naira each depending on the sex. Teenagers with unplanned pregnancies are sometimes lured to clinics and then forced to hand over their babies.

Hassan said the owner of the "illegal baby factory" is likely to face child abuse and human trafficking charges. Buying or selling of babies is illegal in Nigeria and can carry a 14-year jail term.

Raids by the police in 2008 showed an alleged network of such clinics, popularly called baby "farms" or "factories".

This was the second such arrest for Dr. Orikara, who claims that his clinic is an adoption agency where girls with unwanted pregnancies receive help and the children get new parents. But sources described the clinic as a link in a human trafficking ring with infants being "farmed" and sold. He was said to have started the business in Port Harcourt, Rivers State, before relocating to Aba after a botched prosecution following an earlier trial for similar crime.

Inside a Baby Factory

In Lekki [Nigeria], one Mrs. Theresa Marques, 84, owner of an orphanage, sold babies for N100,000 [$633 USD], N200,000 [$1266].

Her home served as a baby factory. A medical doctor was also arrested at the maternity. He was caught in a private room in the hospital with a young lady half naked. He himself was scantily dressed. The woman allegedly harboured young men and women who engaged in sex in order to produce children for her orphanage, which were then sold.

Uduma Kalu,
"How Child Trafficking Network Operates in South East,"
Vanguard *(Lagos), July 30, 2011. www.vanguardngr.com.*

Human Trafficking Is a Major Problem

The rise of baby factories or sale of baby business is fast becoming a menace. Enugu Zonal Head of NAPTIP, Mrs Ijeoma Okoronkwo, said in the southeast alone, the agency has over 40 cases pending in courts with most of them cases of child sales.

It is no longer news that the baby selling business has given rise to the phenomenon of many hitherto childless women pretending to be pregnant after making arrangement with such baby clinics or any willing mother ready to sell her child, and then collecting such babies immediately after birth and announcing to people they just gave birth.

Stories abound of some "alhajas" or big madams even in cities like Lagos and Abuja, who collect girls or willing women in their houses, take care of them till they deliver, and then sell their babies.

Aside from baby factories or clinics, children are still being trafficked from rural areas to cities in the country daily for use in plantations, factories, as house helps, for prostitution or for black magic rituals.

It is interesting to note that some of these girls selling their babies have been sold themselves. They were trafficked from their villages for as small as 2,000 naira by their parents or guardians under the guise of going to work; they become sexual tools for their masters, and some fall victims of rapists . . . and on falling pregnant and being abandoned by their abuser, run to such homes to sell their babies and the cycle goes on.

Stories abound of some "alhajas" or big madams . . . who collect girls or willing women in their houses, take care of them till they deliver, and then sell their babies.

Poverty, trafficking, waywardness on the part of some of these girls who believe the sale of their bodies pays better than other means of livelihood, abusive masters and collaborating madams, wicked relatives who do not care for orphaned children, and greedy men and women are fast killing the motherly love and instinct.

Suffice to add that there is no justification for any woman [even one] of teenage years to sell her own child.

Some of them, especially the pregnant teen girls, may give the excuse that they ran away from home to escape the wrath of their parents, and since they have no means of caring for themselves and the child when born, go to such homes to be cared for and then sell the babies. Some may say they sell the babies because they believe they will be given to childless couples to take care of. You can only be sure of proper care for your child when he or she is adopted through due process and where there are regulations. Anybody with other motives could feign childlessness to buy your baby. Besides there is no detailed information of who the buyers are, where they will live with the child and how they will take care of him or her.

There should be sensitization for girls to take their babies or pregnancies to appropriate government or other approved social welfare centres and desist from baby factories or giving them to every Dick and Harry.

The owners of such baby factories should always be prosecuted to serve as a deterrent to others and the members of the public can help by reporting such baby sellers and buyers. People, especially childless couples, should go to appropriate places to adopt and not contracting women to give birth for them to buy.

Teenagers Should Be Educated

Teenage schoolgirls should be sensitized on preventing unwanted pregnancies and parents should be . . . monitoring their children's conduct, for instance the 32 girls rescued are people's children, the question is, were their parents looking for them or did they know they were at the baby factory and waiting for them to sell the babies and come back?

Those who sell babies because they see the children becoming encumbrances to their lifestyles or getting in the way of their trade should have a rethink as it pays more to keep than sell one's baby.

Government should do more in alleviating poverty in the country, particularly at the grassroots level, and also set up several social welfare centres . . . to take care of poor women or girls who cannot fend for themselves in pregnancy or after birth. All hands must be on deck to sensitize and fight trafficking in persons.

Celebrities Adopt Children from Abroad

Yasmin Alibhai-Brown

In the following viewpoint, Yasmin Alibhai-Brown describes the adoption of a Rwandan refugee by British actors Emma Thompson and her husband, Greg Wise. Alibhai-Brown became acquainted with the family in 2003. In 2009, the boy, Tindyebwa Agaba, graduated from Exeter University. Alibhai-Brown uses this occasion to comment on the generosity and compassion of Thompson's family as well as that of other British celebrities, in contrast to American stars such as Madonna who, in Alibhai-Brown's opinion, adopt internationally out of selfishness. Alibhai-Brown is a Ugandan-born British journalist.

As you read, consider the following questions:

1. How did Alibhai-Brown become acquainted with Tindyebwa Agaba and the family of Emma Thompson and Greg Wise, according to the viewpoint?

2. What was a "tricky" moment in the relationship between Tindy and Emma Thompson's family, according to Alihabi-Brown?

3. As reported by the author, what is the name of Madonna's second adopted child?

Tears welled up when I saw the proud pictures of [British actress] Emma Thompson and [British actor] Greg Wise with their adopted Rwandan refugee son Tindy as he was awarded a politics degree from Exeter University.

How smart he looks in his graduation gear, how safe and open and joyful at last.

Fame Can Be a Blessing

Cynics, be damned: the whole family deserve all the happiness in the world and are an example of how fame, though too often a curse, can be a blessing for those who least expect it.

I have witnessed this story unfolding and have been personally touched by it.

A Courteous Request

It was some three years back that I had a beautifully written and courteous e-mail from someone called Tindyebwa Agaba.

Would Ms Yasmin please find the time to be interviewed on camera for a student project on refugees in Britain?

It went on to explain that he was a refugee from Rwanda, next door to Uganda, my old homeland.

Now, we journalists get a whole pile of such requests every day and often have to decline because of other commitments. But I found it impossible to refuse this request.

Through the anonymity of e-mails, his gentle voice grabbed my attention and would not be ignored.

On the appointed day he came, punctual and polite. Behind him was someone holding some of the equipment, again impeccably good-mannered and self-effacing. It was Greg Wise, I realised with surprise.

Tindy (as he likes to be known) explained he had been adopted by Wise and Emma Thompson after meeting them at a Refugee Council party six years ago when he was a teenager.

He didn't go into much detail then about how much he had been through before this stroke of amazing luck, though I later learned how he had been a child soldier in war-torn Rwanda before charity workers had brought him to Britain.

Back then, he just wanted to talk to me because he knew I defend the rights of refugees and asylum seekers.

The filming done, they packed up and I heard myself saying to Tindy: 'If you want to have a coffee some time, do get in touch.'

To bring an adolescent stranger into your family where there is a young daughter—what's more, to bring a troubled black child into a middle-class white family—was an act of extraordinary courage and optimism.

Building Rapport

And so he did, and so we met and talked and built up a rapport. When times were hard—like when he wasn't sure he would be granted the right to live in Britain permanently—he would e-mail me, just to unburden, but careful never to impose or ask for too much.

Emma Thompson describes how, when she met him for the first time, 'he was an enchanting boy'.

He still is that: slightly built, Puck-like, with bright eyes and a smile that could sell toothpaste.

Last winter when I performed my one-woman show to raise money for refugees, Tindy came up on stage to speak to the audience about his life in Rwanda and the uncertain years here when the authorities would not believe his story.

He had seen hell in Rwanda where genocide and rape suddenly swept through the land, sparing nobody.

His loved ones were among the dead and violated. With such a background, he might have turned wild, vengeful, murderous even.

Yet somehow he kept his hope and grip on good values. Thompson and Wise had faith in themselves—and in him—to turn the future bright.

Madonna and Malawi

Madonna has been loudly criticized, from many sides, for adopting David and Mercy [children from Malawi] in order to publicize herself, and thus treating the children like fashion accessories. This is not the problem. The problem lies rather in the assumption that adoption is a mode of humanitarianism that forms the condition of possibility for the "fashion vs. philanthropy" debate. This assumption is opened for critique in the [John] Sayles film *Casa de los Babys*. . . . In contrast, it is reinforced in the media representations of Madonna's adoptions, positively by her fans as they applaud her actions for their benefit to Malawi and negatively by her critics as they hold up the act of "saving a life" as the standard by which Madonna's adoption should be judged. It is further disseminated in Madonna's film, where adopting a baby is literally presented as an equivalent to writing a check to support other humanitarian projects. Particularly in [the documentary] *I Am Because We Are*, such representations not only consolidate counterproductive visions of transnational adoption but also risk entrenching an anachronistic vision of humanitarianism precisely in the act of trying to reconfigure it.

Kerry Bystrom,
"On 'Humanitarian' Adoption (Madonna in Malawi),"
Humanity, *Fall 2011.*

Their first child, Gaia, had been born after arduous IVF [in vitro fertilisation] treatment, and subsequent attempts to conceive a sibling ended in disappointment.

So when Tindy was introduced to them in 2003, it was perfect providence: He fulfilled their need for another child.

I do find that choice awesome and am not sure I could have done it myself. Having your own sulky teenager is hard enough. To bring an adolescent stranger into your family where there is a young daughter—what's more, to bring a troubled black child into a middle-class white family—was an act of extraordinary courage and optimism.

Tricky Moments

There have been some tricky moments—like when Tindy openly criticised his university for not doing enough to attract nonwhite students.

The media went for him and the furor broke just as he was trying to get full citizenship rights. His parents had to help calm things down.

Throughout it all, Thompson and Wise have behaved with exemplary delicacy and sensitivity and have tried to protect Tindy from the baggage of celeb life.

It wasn't always easy for them, unfairly mocked as they were for being naïve 'luvvies' and 'compassion junkies'. But they are not the only British stars single-minded enough to ignore the sniping in their attempt to help the disadvantaged.

Celebrity Adoptions

[British actor] Colin Firth, his wife, Livia, and mum, Shirley, have spent years helping refugees and those whose rights are denied. So, too, have Harriet Walter, Juliet Stevenson and the many others who support amnesty and liberty.

They seek no glory and use their status and wealth wisely. Unfortunately, that is patently not true of many A-list Americans who have taken to sweeping around the globe, picking up children like curios.

From a sea of wailing souls, they choose the cutest babies on offer, preferably black ones because—as the appalling [character] Bruno says in [British comedian/actor] Sacha Baron Cohen's new film—black goes with everything you wear.

And all the while it is meant to show us they are saving not just the carefully selected children, but the nation they hail from, the continent even.

Many A-list Americans . . . have taken to sweeping around the globe, picking up children like curios.

No humility here, and none of the carefully crafted normality and integrity of the Thompson/Wise family.

I have never heard or seen them use Tindy to parade their compassion in public. Yet that, I fear, is the [main] motivation for [American pop singer] Madonna, the self-crowned Queen of Malawi, whose adoptees seem to be must-have possessions, just as [American pop singer] Michael Jackson's made-to-order children were for him, his toys, to dress and play with as he chose.

It is all wrapped up in the cloth of immaculate virtue, of course, but that can't conceal the greed and arrogance curled up under it.

Of course, Madonna's adopted children, Mercy and David, will have indescribable wealth, a lifestyle from another planet. But will it give them security, stability, serenity, self-reliance, their own identities and self-determination? No, to all those.

The singer appeared to have no qualms about walking out of her most recent marriage, which, whether she ever admits it or not, will rebound on her own birth children, Lourdes and Rocco, as well as adopted son David.

Then with unseemly haste she went on her second adoption spree, for baby Mercy.

The judge who initially refused the application (before the decision was overturned) understood that such flash, high-profile adoptions send out the wrong message and would not necessarily be in the best interests of the child.

But eventually Mercy was duly packaged up and handed over. I hope I am wrong but I do not expect we will ever see family graduation pics of Mercy and David flanked by a mumsy Madonna.

The 'material girl' will give them everything they want and a distorted luxury upbringing.

She wanted them as yet another of her many indulgences and will pass on that acquisitiveness to her sprogs.

Tindy is so much luckier, although his childhood embodies the worst horrors of Africa, far worse than the poverty in Malawi.

He is with a family who expect him to find and make himself, to be what he can be with their support, to resist terrible temptations.

And that picture of his graduation ceremony, surrounded by the family who love him dearly, is the greatest testimony possible to their collective achievements.

That is what adoption should be about—a lesson yet to be learnt by Madonna and those in Hollywood who are following in her foolishly high-heeled footsteps.

Transnational Adoptions Pose Difficult Questions

Elizabeth Larsen

In the following viewpoint, journalist Elizabeth Larsen describes the adoption of her Guatemalan daughter. After adopting the child she and her husband name Flora, the couple realized that Flora's birth mother could have been coerced or lied to in order to force her to give up the child for adoption. The couple hired an investigator to find the birth mother, and the family had a reunion with her in Guatemala City. They discovered the mother was not coerced, but loves her child deeply. Larsen believes adoption is much more complicated ethically than many are willing to admit.

As you read, consider the following questions:

1. Why is Flora's middle name Beatriz, according to the author?

2. According to the viewpoint, what did the adoption lawyer threaten to do if the baby's foster mother, Maria, continued to contact Larsen?

3. Of what was a Utah adoption agency indicted in 2007, according to the viewpoint?

I first met my daughter in the lobby of the Westin Camino Real, the grandest hotel in Guatemala City. The night before, my husband, Walter, and I had soothed our nerves running on the treadmills in the fitness center, where a polite attendant handed us plush white towels and spritzed the equipment with a flowery disinfectant. Afterward I wrote a series of letters to our daughter. Because children adopted from overseas usually have little information about their history, parents are advised to document the trip as best they can, creating what is known as an "adoption story."

Reading the journal now, more than two years later, it feels so self-conscious. "We've been waiting so long to meet you—almost seven months!" the first entry reads. "Ever since you were seven days old and the agency e-mailed us your beautiful photos, we've wondered what you will be like. We fell in love with you that minute!" Gone is any sense of the surreal. Walter and I already had two biological sons; now we were jetting into a third world country with the sole aim of leaving with one of its daughters. (Wanting a girl, we'd opted for the sure bet that adoption offers.) I mentioned, but didn't dwell on, the brutal poverty outside our hotel windows, focusing instead on how my sons were looking forward to meeting their little sister.

A Spark of Shame

There is one section of the journal, however, that jumps out from the boilerplate. "I feel so sad for the pain your birth mother must be in since she is not able to raise you," I wrote. "But I believe now that I am your 'real' mommy." Reading those words now sparks a flash of shame. Because even though my daughter was, as is required by U.S. immigration law, legally classified as an orphan, she had two Guatemalan parents who were very much alive.

I remember being comforted by the Guatemalan social worker's report on the case; the baby's mother, Beatriz, had evidently made an informed choice to place her for adoption. Or at least that's what I told myself.

The truth is that I didn't know Beatriz. And I was secretly relieved this was so. . . .

Walter and I had tried to do everything right. We'd heard of corrupt adoption lawyers, fly-by-night operators who use online photo listings to lure parents, of baby stealing and baby selling, and of the myriad agencies that offer, for hefty fees, to help Americans bring home a child from some of the world's poorest countries. We chose one of the largest and most respected, and faithfully attended all the counseling appointments it offered, including a seminar that featured a session with an American birth mother. She clearly loved her son, but said she hadn't been ready to become a mother. "I'm not his parent," she told us.

And yet when it came time to choose a program, our agency told us to go with whatever we were comfortable with, as if "open" and "closed" were items on a menu. We asked our social worker about a domestic open adoption; she said that because we already had biological children and were only open to adopting a girl, we wouldn't be a very compelling family to an American birth mother. We never discussed adopting from the U.S. foster care system or an Eastern European orphanage; we wanted a baby who had never spent an hour in institutionalized care. We also wanted our daughter's country of origin to be easy to travel to, so we could go there for family vacations. Talk about menu items!

Moral Questions

We did agonize over some moral questions—the potential hardships for a Latina child raised in a white family, the ethics of choosing the sex of our child. At every step, we were reassured that what we were doing was a good and worthy thing. "I think [adoption] is almost an antithesis to oppression," Kevin Kreutner, a moderator at the support group Guatadopt .com who is in contact with his children's Guatemalan family, told me. "For people who are given no access to family planning, have an unplanned pregnancy, and can't raise that child, there is a liberating sense where they can realize that this child will not suffer that same oppression."

"I just need to know that the child we adopt has no other options," Walter finally told our social worker. I can't remember her exact answer, but it was something along the lines of "all these children need families." When I later told this to an adoptee-rights advocate, she said the agency should have pursued a discussion that might have dissuaded us from transnational adoption, or led us to a program through which we could sponsor a child to remain with her family. But the truth is I don't think I would have listened—so absorbed was I in the force of my own wanting.

When we got our daughter's paperwork, Walter and I noticed that her first, middle, and last names were exactly the same as her mother's. We told ourselves this was probably because the adoption lawyer had suggested it—an efficient decision made for the sake of checkups and court appearances. I'd read that some adoptees believe their given name is a precious connection to their heritage. When we asked our social worker what she thought about changing it, she said it was up to us to decide what was right for our family. So we changed her first name to Flora and made Beatriz her middle name.

We did agonize over some moral questions—the potential hardships for a Latina child raised in a white family, the ethics of choosing the sex of our child.

We did not, however, want Flora's life before us to be irretrievable, so we asked if Beatriz wanted to meet us and stay in touch. Our social worker contacted the lawyer in Guatemala, who replied that Beatriz "would love to know us." Then, a week before our trip, the social worker called and said there would be no meeting; Beatriz had gone back to her village and wasn't reachable.

"But she's from Guatemala City," I said. "Do you think the lawyer is telling us the truth?" The social worker said it was hard to know. Adoptions in Guatemala are arranged entirely by private lawyers, without oversight from any central authority, and corruption is widespread. Our agency promised it carefully screened those it worked with in Guatemala. But this incident gave us pause. The lawyer might technically be representing both Flora and us, but whose interests was he really looking out for?

A Sinking Heart

A week later, we flew to Guatemala City. The hotel of choice for American adoptive parents is the Marriott, which is so used to these "pickup" trips, it offers strollers for rent and has arranged with a nearby pharmacy to deliver formula and diapers to panicky new parents. Via chat rooms, adoptive parents with similar pickup trip schedules make arrangements to connect at the Marriott. But the idea of all that camaraderie just heightened my anxiety. So we stayed at the Westin.

As the elevator chugged down toward the lobby, Walter pointed the video camera at me and said, "Here's Mommy waiting to see Flora for the first time!" I forced a feeble smile. I was naked and sweating when I met my sons in the sterile glow of a hospital birthing room. Now I stepped out onto rose-marble floors to face Flora's foster mother Maria, a stout woman with a six-month-old girl riding at her hip in a woven sling. As they cuddled and laughed—later I'd look at photos of this moment to remind myself that Flora could laugh; for weeks her eyes gazed [at] her new home with a dull blankness—my heart sank. . . .

The Birth Mother Makes Contact

Maria called on Flora's first birthday to say that Beatriz wanted us to know she felt she had made the right decision. A few weeks later, our social worker told us that Beatriz had visited the lawyer and wanted to see photos of her daughter.

Several months later, Maria called again. The lawyer had threatened to fire her if she continued to contact us.

That night I was changing Flora's diaper. "Who's my girl?" I sang as I pulled the tab taut across her stomach. She pointed at her chest and laughed, her dimples creasing into pinholes. Then she reached up to tickle my chin. "Flora Beatriz," I cooed. "You are one beautiful kid." Hearing myself say her middle name took me aback. Beatriz, I suddenly realized, had chosen it, the only connection to their brief life together.

Is it ethical for an adoptive parent to push for information about her child's birth family? Or should that be a decision left to the adoptee?

And that's when it finally sank in: Beatriz hadn't made a "choice" in the liberating way that our post-*Roe* [referring to *Roe v. Wade*, the court ruling allowing women to have abortions] culture thinks about reproductive options. Like any woman in the developing world placing a child for adoption, she'd buckled under crushing financial or social pressure— perhaps even coercion. I'd considered this before, but had always batted the thought away by telling myself that Flora was going to be adopted, whether it was we who stepped forward or someone else.

Walter walked in, flushed and sweating from wrestling with the boys, who were now happily digging into bowls of applesauce.

"She's getting so big," he said. "She'll be talking soon."

His smile fell as he saw me crying. "Did something happen today?" I nodded.

"I think Beatriz wants us to find her," was all I could say.

Is it ethical for an adoptive parent to push for information about her child's birth family? Or should that be a decision left to the adoptee? And what about the birth family's right to privacy? . . .

Some of these reunions could turn out to be unsettling. "One of the ways that wrongdoers hide their child laundering schemes is by the closed adoption system," says David Smolin, a law professor who's written extensively on corruption in transnational adoption. He and his wife adopted two sisters from India only to find out that they had been stolen from their birth family. Last March [2007] a Utah adoption agency was indicted in an alleged fraud scheme involving 81 Samoan children whose parents were told that they were sending their children away to take advantage of opportunities in the United States—that there would be letters, photos, and visits, and that the children would return when they turned 18. . . .

Finding Beatriz

I was working on deadline the afternoon Susi's e-mail flashed on my screen, a month after we had hired her to find Beatriz. Operating by word of mouth, Susi has done hundreds of searches for birth families in Guatemala and elsewhere in Central America. In 1999, when she first considered this line of work, "I asked my friends and they all said, 'No, don't get involved in that.' People here see adoptions only as a business. A big business. And when there is a lot of money involved, there is corruption."

Still, the idea of connecting families appealed to her. Her first search was easy. "I knocked on the door of the address I was given by the adoptive family and the birth mother opened the door." Soon, though, she got threats: Stop, or you'll get into trouble. Her husband accompanies her on every search; she will not contact anyone who works directly with adoptions, or discuss the details of a search.

Her e-mail relieved us of two worries: Beatriz had been hoping we would find her, and she had not been coerced into placing Flora for adoption. She thanked us for making it possible to watch her child grow up. She missed her, prayed for her, and wanted Flora to know that not a day passed when she didn't think about her. She said that before the adoption she was a bubbly person. Now she kept mostly to herself.

I'd nurtured a vague notion of a faraway woman grieving for her lost child. But as soon as an image of Beatriz sobbing into her pillow materialized, my brain concocted a counter-narrative, a story in which she was healing from her loss. A story in which not having to raise the child I tucked into bed every night freed Beatriz in some way.

Then one evening not long after the e-mail arrived, Walter and I spent our date night at a reading of *Outsiders Within: Writing on Transracial Adoption*, an anthology that is a stirring and stern rebuke to the standard heartwarming adoption narrative. Back in our car, Walter bowed his head.

"We should give her back," he said.

I'd harbored the same thought, but the anguish on his face threatened me enough to push back.

"We can't," I answered.

"Why not?" he countered. "It wouldn't take much money to support them."

"Because we are her family."

"She'd adjust."

"How do you know that?" It was an unconvincing dodge. We were friends with several families who had adopted toddlers; their kids were thriving. "How could we do that to the boys?" I insisted.

"We couldn't," Walter said.

"And how could we do that to us? I couldn't live with that pain."

"But why should Beatriz have to?" he asked.

A Different Computation

To most Americans, Flora's adoption is measured entirely by what she gains—Montessori schools, soccer camps, piano lessons, college. But it no longer quite computes that way for me. To gain a family, my daughter had to lose a family. To become an American child, she had to stop being a Guatemalan child.

[Hollee] McGinnis [policy and operations director of the Evan B. Donaldson Adoption Institute] told me that because adoptive parents are put through such a rigmarole of assessments and trainings, it's easy for them to jump on the "super-parent track" in the quest to raise a happy child. "If 'adoptees want to know their past' becomes another item on the super-parent track, it's important to understand whether you are doing a search because you don't want your child to be mad at you later," she says. "My research has shown what makes a healthy identity is when the adopted person feels like they have a chance to make decisions."

Walter and I are nothing if not grade-grubbing students in the super-parent classroom. We have a babysitter who is from Guatemala and speaks only Spanish with our children. She cooks us pepian and invites us for tamales with her family, which likes my tres leches cake. A jade statue of a Mayan corn goddess stands on our living room shelf, and a woven huipil hangs in the hall. We send the boys to a summer camp for children adopted from Latin America and their siblings, and get together once a month with other families with Guatemalan children. From the moment we met Flora, we planned on visiting Guatemala every few years.

To gain a family, my daughter had to lose a family. To become an American child, she had to stop being a Guatemalan child.

Which is all very well—but the results can sometimes feel like a trip to Epcot. Perhaps one day Flora will appreciate our efforts; maybe she will resent them. I hope that if she rolls her eyes at our jaguar masks and woven placemats, I'll be able to smile. But what if the decision she most resents is the one we can't rescind? You can't exactly put a birth family back into a drawer.

By the time we returned to Guatemala City, Flora was two and a half. Walter and I had decided it would be easier for her to meet Beatriz this young; as she grew up, she and Beatriz would figure out what they wanted from their relationship. But it was an uneasy compromise. Unlike our domestic counterparts, we didn't have the benefit of longitudinal studies and books detailing best practices. We didn't even really have an open adoption. There was no legal document to set out the terms of contact, only a tendril of trust spun from the fact that Beatriz, Walter, and I all loved the same child. . . .

A Meeting at McDonald's

Susi had decided we should meet Beatriz at McDonald's because it would afford us some anonymity. It turned out to be the perfect setting for Flora, no stranger to the pleasures of McNuggets and giant sliding tubes. In the lunchtime rush, few looked up from their Big Macs to wonder why a blonde gringa and a petite Guatemalan were clinging to each other and weeping.

When you meet your daughter's mother, you don't waste time with small talk. And at first, there was no need for talking because Beatriz could not take her eyes off Flora.

"Hola, mi amor," she said as she bent down.

Flora frowned and turned away. "I want Daddy," she said.

Walter picked her up and kissed her cheek. "Sweetie," he said. "This is Beatriz. She's your Guatemalan mommy." Flora buried her face in his shoulder. Nervously, we tried to draw her out. But Beatriz told us not to worry.

With Susi translating, Beatriz told us that she was deeply depressed for a year after the adoption was finalized. She got through her pain by turning to God. She loved being in the hospital with Flora and demanded as a condition of the adoption that she could visit her in foster care. She assumed that she would never see Flora again and she was still in shock that she had. She took obvious delight in how healthy and happy Flora was. She told us the names of all of Flora's relatives and explained that Flora gets her dimples from her uncle. . . .

A Complicated Privilege

At the end of our third hour together, all of us—save Flora—looked shell-shocked, but no one wanted to leave. Beatriz asked if I worked. I said I was a journalist and that one day I hoped to write about women in Guatemala and other countries who place their children for adoption. I told her that we don't hear much about these mothers.

Beatriz nodded. "Please write about me," she said. "Please tell the Americans how much I love my daughter."

To fall so deeply for a daughter who has no genetic link to me made me realize that we are simply hardwired to love the children we are given to raise.

So what will Flora make of that day, much less this [viewpoint]? I have no idea. But I think a lot about what Hollee McGinnis told me about her Korean family. "Adoptees have to ultimately figure out what it means that they were adopted," she said. "Yes, they can go and ask some questions, but the meaning-making will be theirs. Openness is really good in that you don't have to jump through all these extra hurdles. But the work of figuring it out is still there."

Loving an adopted child is easy. In fact, Flora's adoption was in some astonishing way more powerful than giving birth to my sons. To fall so deeply for a daughter who has no genetic link to me made me realize that we are simply hardwired to love the children we are given to raise.

Raising an adopted child is, however, a complicated privilege. Walter and I could not turn our backs on Beatriz's poverty. After trying unsuccessfully to find a nonprofit that would help us sponsor her somehow, we finally decided to just send her money through Susi so she could finish her education. Could this encourage women in her neighborhood to place a child for adoption? Could we possibly not do it?

What I do know is that I have never felt more like Flora's "real" mother than when Beatriz and I were holding each other next to Ronald McDonald. And that's not because Flora so obviously saw me as her mommy. It's because I now understand I'm not her only one.

Periodical Bibliography

The following articles have been selected to supplement the diverse views presented in this chapter.

Scott Carney   "Meet the Parents: Nageswar Rao and Sivagama Say a Boy Being Raised in the Midwest Was Stolen from Them in the Slums of Chennai," *Mother Jones*, vol. 34, no. 2, March–April 2009.

Kim Do-hyun   "Overseas Adoption: Child Welfare or Abuse?," *Korea Times*, December 30, 2011.

Scott Farwell   "Open Hearts, Closed Doors," *Dallas Morning News*, March 27, 2011.

Jeremy Laurance   "The Big Question: Is It Exploitation to Adopt Children from the Developing World?," *Independent* (London), October 6, 2006.

Caroline Overington   "Adopting a Hard Line on Parents," *Australian* (Sydney), February 9, 2010.

Charlotte Paulsen and Joseph R. Merighi   "Adoption Preparedness, Cultural Engagement, and Parental Satisfaction in Intercountry Adoption," *Adoption Quarterly*, vol. 12, no. 1, January 2009.

Laurie Penny   "Profit, Not Care: The Ugly Side of Overseas Adoptions," *Independent* (London), June 16, 2011.

Ginger Thompson   "After Haiti Quake, the Chaos of U.S. Adoptions," *New York Times*, August 4, 2010.

Henry Ugboaja   "Africa: U.S. Families Adoption of Children, for Trade or Charity?," *Daily Independent* (Lagos), June 29, 2010.

Daniel B. Wood   "Returned Russian Child Spotlights International Adoption Problems," *Christian Science Monitor*, April 13, 2010.

GLOBALVIEWPOINTS

CHAPTER 3

Gender, Race, and Indigenous Peoples

Girls Are Given Up for Adoption More Often than Boys in China

Jacob Sullum

In the following viewpoint, Jacob Sullum argues that the Chinese government's population policy leads to the loss of daughters for that country. In China, he explains, couples are allowed one child; however, if the first child is a girl, they are allowed a second pregnancy to try for a boy. Second daughters are nearly always put up for adoption, often internationally. As a result, according to Sullum, China is suffering from a serious gender imbalance that will lead to large numbers of young Chinese men without wives. Consequently, international adoptions are being curtailed. Sullum is the senior editor at Reason *magazine.*

As you read, consider the following questions:

1. According to the viewpoint, how many informal adoptions occur in China each year? How many registered adoptions occur in China each year?
2. How does the Chinese government explain the gender imbalance, according to Sullum?

Jacob Sullum, "Thank Deng Xiaoping for Little Girls: The Tyrannical Roots of China's International Adoption Program," *Reason* magazine, vol. 39, no. 7, December 2007, p. 40.

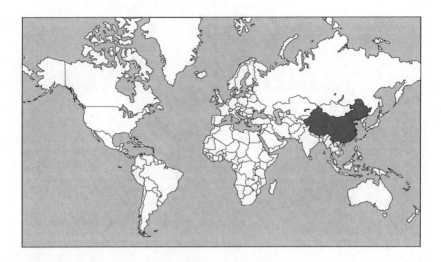

3. What are some of the new stricter criteria for American adoptive parents imposed by the Chinese government, according to the author?

A s I gradually realized, the truth about Chinese adoption is more complicated than the conventional story about Westerners who magnanimously take in China's unwanted girls. It's not much of an exaggeration to say these girls are "unwanted" only because the Chinese government has made them so. Although the government's oppressive, family-destroying policies have had the incidental benefit of bringing joy to the lives of adoptive parents in the U.S. and elsewhere, it will be a great victory for liberty when such heartwarming stories stop appearing on newsstands and bookshelves. These adoptions would not be occurring if the Chinese government did not try to dictate the most basic and intimate of life's decisions.

In 2006 about 6,500 Chinese girls were adopted by Americans. Roughly the same number were adopted by people in other Western countries, including Canada, Spain, Germany, France, and the U.K. But these 13,000 girls were just a fraction of China's abandoned children, the vast majority of whom are female. The Chinese government has estimated there are 160,000 orphans in China at any given time; in her 2000 adoption memoir, *The Lost Daughters of China*, California journalist Karin Evans notes that human rights activists say the number of orphans "is undoubtedly far higher—perhaps ten times the official count, or more." Between a government that is not known for its openness and outside observers who are forced to guesstimate (and who may have their own reasons for exaggerating), the relevant figures are maddeningly hard to pin down. . . .

Chinese Girls Are Not Unwanted

Contrary to the impression that abandoned Chinese girls are unwanted, many of them are adopted domestically. [Professor of Asian studies Kay Ann] Johnson notes that adoption—of girls as well as boys—is firmly rooted in Chinese tradition. Indeed, historically it was more accepted in China than it was until recently in the U.S. Johnson reports that the Chinese government registered more than 56,000 domestic adoptions in 2000, about 11,000 from state-run orphanages, the rest "foundlings adopted [directly] from society." She believes informal adoptions dwarf the official numbers, perhaps totaling half a million or more each year in the late 1980s, when registered adoptions ranged between 10,000 and 15,000 annually.

These informally adopted children, overwhelmingly girls, never make it to orphanages and are instead raised by kindly strangers or by friends, neighbors, acquaintances, or relatives of their parents without the government's blessing. Because such adoptions are not officially recognized, the children are not eligible for a bukou, the residence permit that allows access to school and other benefits. In addition to the hardships associated with lack of a bukou and the expense of raising another child, couples who adopt informally risk penalties for skirting limits on family size. But they take the girls in anyway.

Chinese Family-Size Restrictions

Surprisingly, until 1999 Chinese couples who wanted to adopt faced the same family-size restrictions as couples who wanted to reproduce. Those restrictions, known loosely as the "one-child" policy, were first imposed in 1979 by Chinese paramount leader Deng Xiaoping and are still in force. Deng was convinced that curbing population growth was a precondition for prosperity, although demographers generally find that the relationship runs in the opposite direction, with people choosing to have fewer children as they become more affluent.

Contrary to the impression that abandoned Chinese girls are unwanted, many of them are adopted domestically. [Asian studies professor Kay Ann] Johnson notes that adoption—of girls as well as boys—is firmly rooted in Chinese tradition.

From the beginning, there were exceptions to the one-child rule. For example, members of 55 officially recognized non-Han Chinese minorities, who together represent about 8 percent of the population, have always been allowed two children per family. The limits tend to be tighter in cities than in rural areas, where some 75 percent of the population lives. Beginning in the mid-1980s, most provinces adopted a "one-son/ two-child" policy, which allows a couple whose first child is a daughter to try again for a son. In addition to the variation in official rules, there is wide variation in enforcement, both over time and from one locale to another. In some places and times, Johnson reports, unauthorized pregnancies prompt crushing fines, mandatory sterilization, and forced late-term abortions. In others, local officials may look the other way or back down in response to the pleading of parents or the anger of their neighbors.

This sort of give and take was apparent in May [2007], when a population control crackdown in the Guangxi autonomous region provoked rioting in which "as many as 3,000 people stormed government offices, overturned vehicles, burned documents, and confronted officials," according to a *New York Times* report. Residents were angry about fines and compulsory abortions aimed at enforcing family-size limits that evidently had been ignored for years. A local official, even while blaming the unrest on "backward ideas about birth control and the rule of law," conceded that "it's also possible that problems exist in the government's birth control work." Another local official told Reuters the government's response to over-quota pregnancies and births, which included destroying the homes of parents who failed to pay heavy fines within three days, "got out of hand"; he promised "the methods will be adjusted."

> *Given the barriers to adoption in China, its frequency . . . is impressive evidence that, far from being unwanted in the country of their birth, China's daughters are highly valued.*

Strict Adoption Laws

You might assume, as I did, that the government would waive family-size limits for couples volunteering to raise children who would otherwise become (or remain) wards of the state. But officials worried that making adoption easier would indirectly encourage more births by allowing parents who had hit the legal limit on children to give a girl up (or pretend to do so) and try again for a boy. So until China's adoption law was changed in 1999, adoptive parents had to be over 35 and childless (except for parents willing to adopt disabled children). Even now, adoptive parents have to be over 30, and couples who already have children can adopt only from orphanages, where just a small minority of the country's foundlings end up. In the U.S., by contrast, there are no uniform restrictions on parents' ages or the number of children they may adopt. The rules vary from state to state and depend on whether the adoption is carried out privately or through a state-run foster care system.

Given the barriers to adoption in China, its frequency, once informal adoptions are taken into account, is impressive evidence that, far from being unwanted in the country of their birth, China's daughters are highly valued. It's true that China's strong patriarchal traditions, according to which sons carry on the family line while daughters become members of other families when they marry, mean parents are anxious to have at least one boy. Especially in rural areas, parents value a boy's superior strength and expect sons, more so than daughters, to support them in their old age. These long-standing attitudes explain why boys are rarely abandoned in China and rarely end up in orphanages. But the surveys Johnson and her colleagues have conducted in rural China indicate that parents already believe girls are nice too, as the government's heavy-handed propaganda aims to convince them. (Johnson's book includes a photograph of a building bearing the slogan, "Daughters Are Also Descendants.") The idea that a complete family requires at least one boy and one girl is quite common, Johnson says, and many rural parents perceive daughters as more caring and attentive than sons. . . .

Although the government prefers to blame the problem solely on the backward gender preferences of Chinese peasants, it seems clear that "the current political situation" results in hundreds of thousands of abandonments each year by parents who otherwise would have kept these children. Evans and Johnson both note that the imposition of stricter population controls in a particular area is predictably followed by an increase in the number of abandoned babies. Limits on family size also encourage sex-selective abortions, which are illegal in China but still widespread. Couples who do not have access to ultrasound machines for determining the sex of their unborn children sometimes opt for infanticide instead.

China Imposes Restrictions on International Adoption

Some of the requirements for US couples adopting a child from China include the following:

- Married couples who are between the ages of 30 and 49 can adopt a child from China.

- Couples must be married for at least two years; if either spouse is in a second marriage, the couple must be married for at least five years.

- Each spouse must have at least a high school diploma.

- The family must have a net worth of at least $80,000.

- Morbidly obese people (BMI 40 or greater) are prohibited from adopting a Chinese child.

- If either spouse is blind in one eye or has paralysis of any limb, the couple may not adopt a Chinese child.

- Anyone charged with driving under the influence within the previous five years may not adopt a child from China.

- Parents whose religious beliefs prohibit any type of medical treatment may not adopt.

- Families with five or more children living in the household may not adopt a Chinese child.

Compiled by the editor.

A Serious Gender Imbalance

Meanwhile, China is experiencing a serious gender imbalance. The government acknowledges this problem, although it does not concede that its population policy has anything to do with it. "According to the fifth national census conducted in 2000," the government-operated *China Daily* reported in 2004 . . . "the ratio of newborn males per 100 females in China has reached 119.2, much higher than the normal level of between 103 [and] 107." The official explanation: "Gender discrimination against females is quite common in many rural and underdeveloped areas, which has led to artificial choice of newborn babies' gender by ultrasonic wave. This has reduced the number of female newborn babies."

The Chinese government is asking for trouble by continuing to pursue a population policy that makes girls disappear.

According to United Nations development official Khalid Malik, the newborn gender gap could result in something like 60 million "missing" females by the end of the decade, which amounts to about 2 million per year in the three decades since the Chinese government began enforcing population controls. The International Planned Parenthood Federation estimates that 7 million abortions are performed in China each year and that 70 percent of the aborted fetuses are female. That's 4.9 million girls who are not born, vs. 2.1 million boys, implying an annual difference of 2.8 million. Assuming Planned Parenthood's estimate is in the fight ballpark, it seems that sex-selective abortions are enough on their own to explain China's gender imbalance.

The task of calculating the gender gap is complicated by China's "hidden" population, which includes illegal, over-quota children and informally adopted foundlings. The existence of this population, whose size is by definition unknown, casts doubt on the reliability of the official census data, which may be missing millions of girls. And here's one more complication: In a 2005 *Journal of Political Economy* article, University of Chicago economist Emily Oster argues that hepatitis B infection in mothers, which seems to favor male over female births, may account for as much as 75 percent of China's "missing women."

Assuming the gender gap is real (and whether or not Oster is right about the role of hepatitis B), China is facing a sizable and growing population of young men who have no prospect of marrying and settling down, a situation conducive to crime and political unrest—which, as far as the Chinese government is concerned, are one and the same. In August *China Daily* quoted Chinese officials and academics who blamed "an increasing crime rate, growing demand for pornography, and illegal [forced] marriage" on the disproportionate number of young, single men. "The phenomenon will affect social stability and harmony," warned Zhang Weiqing, head of the National Population and Family Planning Commission.

Even if much of the apparent gender imbalance is due to "hidden" girls missed by the census, driving so many children underground creates an underclass of officially nonexistent people. Either way, the Chinese government is asking for trouble by continuing to pursue a population policy that makes girls disappear.

Far from regretting that policy's unintended consequences, the Chinese government is fiercely proud of its population control efforts: The Chinese envoy to a recent environmental conference bragged that his country's family-size limits have helped ameliorate global warming by preventing some 300 million births. Short of rescinding its population controls, which is what a decent respect for human rights demands, the Chinese government should at least remove the legal obstacles that make it harder for abandoned girls to find homes. It should recognize the informal adoptions that already have occurred and remove the continuing restrictions on domestic adoptions that do not involve orphanages. But the government seems to fear that such changes would be seen as a green light to produce more children.

International Adoptions Are Kept Low

Chinese officials may even be having second thoughts about international adoptions, which account for a small portion of abandoned girls but contribute (slightly) to the gender imbalance and could be seen as indirectly encouraging over-quota births. The number of Chinese babies adopted by Americans peaked at nearly 8,000 in 2005, falling to 6,500 last year. In December 2006 the Chinese government, which already rejected gay couples seeking to adopt, announced new, stricter criteria for adoptive parents that exclude, among others, single people, people older than 50, people with body mass indexes of 40 or more (equivalent to a weight of 271 pounds for someone who is five feet, nine inches tall), people with physical handicaps, people who take drugs for depression or other "severe mental disorders," people with assets below $80,000, and divorced people who have been married to their new spouses for less than five years.

According to the *New York Times*, "The restrictions are in response to an enormous spike in applications by foreigners, which has far exceeded the number of available babies." Since the number of Chinese children who need parents at any given time ranges somewhere between 160,000 (per the government) and 1.6 million (per human rights groups), it seems the demand exceeds the supply only because the government has arbitrarily decided that a small fraction of the children are "available."

Could it be that the children who are deemed unavailable are so sickly or disabled that no one wants to adopt them? Foreigners do adopt "special needs" children from China, and in those cases the government relaxes its criteria a bit, allowing parents as old as 55. In any event, Johnson's research suggests the vast majority of abandoned Chinese girls do not have serious disabilities. At the Hubei orphanage she studied, the proportion of children identified as handicapped fell from 98 percent in the early 1970s to 20 percent in 1992, corresponding to the abandonment of healthy girls that accompanied the population controls imposed in 1979. The "handicapped" category, Johnson notes, "is broadly defined to include many minor problems," such as prominent birthmarks.

Concern about exacerbating China's gender imbalance and embarrassment about seeking foreign parents to raise Chinese girls are . . . plausible explanations for the government's decision to restrict overseas adoptions.

For reasons of its own, apparently, the Chinese government wants to keep the number of international adoptions far lower than it could be. Although cynics might suspect the government is deliberately driving up the price of Chinese babies by restricting the supply, the fees charged to adoptive parents have remained pretty much the same in recent years. Furthermore, Johnson notes, this money, while significant to the middle-class parents who hand it over and to the orphanages that get a share of it, is a drop in the bucket of the Chinese economy. Based on estimated in-country fees of $8,000 and 13,000 adoptions (the 2006 number), the revenue amounts to perhaps $100 million a year. (Foreigners coming to pick up babies represent a very small percentage of China's nearly 100 million annual visitors, so the economic impact of the adoption program is minor even if you consider the additional tourism revenue it brings, which in any event would support the case for expanding international adoptions rather than restricting them.) Concern about exacerbating China's gender imbalance and embarrassment about seeking foreign parents to raise Chinese girls are more plausible explanations for the government's decision to restrict overseas adoptions.

Despite a Federal Law, American Indian Children Are Not Placed with Native Families for Adoption

Lara Marlowe

In the following viewpoint, Irish journalist Lara Marlowe reports on the practice in the United States to take American Indian children from their families to be placed for adoption. The adoptions are generally by white couples, despite a federal law requiring that every effort be made to place American Indian children in Native families. Marlowe argues that federal funding for foster care provides the motivation for states such as South Dakota to confiscate Indian children. Marlowe writes for the Irish Times.

As you read, consider the following questions:

1. As reported by the author, what percentage of all American Indian children were separated from their families and put in institutions according to US government studies in 1969 and 1974?

2. How much money does a state receive when an American Indian child is moved from foster care to adoption, according to the viewpoint?

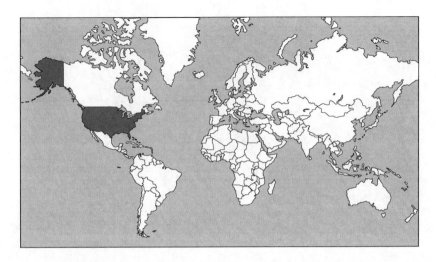

3. What was Dennis Daugaard's job before he became governor of South Dakota, according to Marlowe? Why does Citizens for Responsibility and Ethics in Washington consider Daugaard's positions a conflict of interest?

One night in 2009, a social worker telephoned Janice Howe, a Native American in South Dakota, to tell her that her grandchildren would be taken away because Howe's daughter, Erin Yellow Robe, was about to be arrested for drug use.

Howe was stunned. She had never seen any sign of a drug problem. But the next morning, a social worker arrived to take Yellow Robe's year-old twin babies.

"They were sitting in the car," Howe told National Public Radio [NPR] in a three-part investigative report on the virtual abduction of American Indian children by authorities in South Dakota which was broadcast this week [October 2011]. "They were just looking at me. Because you know most babies don't cry if they're raised in a secure environment.

"So I went out there and took their diaper bags. And they left." White officials have been wresting Indian children from their families since the late 19th century. For a hundred years, the children were lodged in boarding schools where they were often mistreated and abused. Kill the Indian, Save the Man, ran the schools' motto.

The Struggle to Preserve Traditions

Poverty, alcoholism and crime remain serious problems on US Indian reservations. Families are large, but closely knit. And they struggle to preserve tradition. Prejudice against Native Americans is deeply instilled; the Declaration of Independence refers to them as the inhabitants of our frontiers, the merciless Indian savages. US government studies in 1969 and 1974 found that up to 35 per cent of all Native American children were separated from their families and put in institutions, foster or adoptive homes. In 1978, then president Jimmy Carter signed the Indian Child Welfare Act, which established federal standards to protect the children. The act specifies that every attempt must be made to place children with relatives, within their tribe or at the very least, with other Native Americans.

White officials have been wresting Indian children from their families since the late 19th century. For a hundred years, the children were lodged in boarding schools where they were often mistreated and abused.

But the legislation has not been enforced in South Dakota, where only a handful of the 700 Native American children taken annually from their families are placed in Indian homes. NPR found evidence that dozens of Indian families who asked to receive foster children were denied custody. Although Native American children comprise less than 15 per cent of the child population in South Dakota, they make up more than half the children in foster care.

On that day in 2009 when her twin babies were taken, Erin Yellow Robe and her mother Janice Howe sat on the steps and cried. They wondered why the social worker left Yellow Robe's older daughters, Rashauna, then 5, and Antoinette, 6.

The police never came for Yellow Robe. NPR learned from a source who had access to the file that there was merely a rumour, started by someone who didn't like the family, that Yellow Robe abused prescription medication.

Two months after the babies were taken, a social worker took Rashauna and Antoinette from school, without telling their mother and grandmother. Howe waited for them at the school bus stop that day, in vain. The Department of Social Services would not tell her anything. The state government did not answer her letters. When she appealed to the Indian child welfare director, he told her there was nothing he could do. In desperation, Howe asked the social worker to at least place her grandchildren with Native Americans, so they could learn rituals like the ceremonial sauna called sweats and the religious sun dance. Nothing happened.

Months passed before Howe and Yellow Robe were allowed to visit the girls. Howe was upset to see that the girls' long black hair, which she loved plaiting, had been cut, a rite which usually marks death in a Dakota Indian family. The girls were thin and begged to go home. Pray hard, Howe told the girls. Grandma's going to get you back. I don't know how, but grandma's going to get you back. When you start feeling bad, pray or look outside because we're both looking at the same sky.

The Children Are Returned

When the state put Yellow Robe's four children up for adoption, Howe went to her tribe's council, which passed an unprecedented resolution warning the state government that if the children were not returned, the tribe would press charges against the state government for kidnapping. A few weeks later, 18 months after the twins had been taken, a car deliv-

The Indian Child Welfare Act

One of the laws that the United States enacted to preserve the rights of Indian children is the Indian Child Welfare Act (ICWA). On November 8, 1978, Congress passed ICWA in response to the "rising concern . . . over the consequences to Indian children, Indian families, and Indian tribes of abusive child welfare practices that resulted in the separation of large numbers of Indian children from their families and tribes through adoption and foster care placement." By limiting states' powers over Indian children, ICWA aims to support Indian families, specifically by maintaining Indian children with Indian caregivers, while honoring a rich cultural tradition and tribal sovereignty. . . .

In the late 1800s, federal policy makers targeted Indian children as the agents of change in an era when Indian people were perceived as "savages" who needed to be rehabilitated and Christianized in order to survive in an increasingly dominant non-Indian society. Transforming Indian children was perceived as the key to Indian survival in that dominant society, and as a result they were oftentimes removed from their parents and placed in boarding schools where they were denied the right to speak their Native languages, practice their spiritual beliefs, or even adhere to their traditional grooming and attire.

Because they were oftentimes the legal guinea pigs for an assortment of notions regarding the future of Indian tribes and their people, a wealth of unique laws and policies flowered simultaneously with their upbringing. . . . Congress, when it enacted ICWA, recognized that Indian tribes should determine the destiny of their children, and has passed several laws designed to protect this tribal prerogative.

B.J. Jones, "Differing Concepts of 'Permanency': The Adoption and Safe Families Act and the Indian Child Welfare Act,"
Facing the Future: The Indian Child Welfare Act at 30,
eds. Matthew L.M. Fletcher, Wenona T. Singel, and Kathryn E. Fort.
East Lansing: Michigan State University Press, 2009.

ered all four children to Howe's home, without explanation or apology, and with the warning that they could be taken again at any time.

Howe told NPR that the twin babies appeared to have been well treated, but the girls had lost a dress size and were traumatised. When Rashauna wet her pants, Antoinette said, their foster parents forced her to wear the wet pants on her head. The girls hoard food and hide when a car pulls up. Like their mother, they are afraid of white people.

Money is the incentive behind the mass confiscation of American Indian children. A poor state, South Dakota receives $100 million a year from the federal government for the care of foster children. When children are moved from foster care to adoption, the state receives a $4,000 bonus, which is tripled if the child has special needs. South Dakota 10 years ago designated all Indian children special needs.

A private group called Children's Home Society now has a near monopoly on the foster care business in South Dakota. It vets foster homes, trains caseworkers and foster parents, and examines children alleged to have been abused.

Money is the incentive behind the mass confiscation of American Indian children.

Before he became governor of South Dakota in January this year [2011], Dennis Daugaard was paid $115,000 a year as executive director of Children's Home Society. He served as lieutenant governor of the state through the same years, during which the society took in more than $50 million in federal funding. The Citizens for Responsibility and Ethics in Washington group denounced the setup as a massive conflict of interest.

One month ago, both houses of Congress passed the Child and Family Services Improvement and Innovation Act. It promises to maintain federal funding for states like South Dakota, if only they will reduce the number of children in foster care.

Australian Aboriginal Children Were Wrongly Taken from Their Families for Adoption

Catherine Naylor

In the following viewpoint, Australian journalist Catherine Naylor explores the issue of the Stolen Generations, several generations of Aboriginal children taken from their families as recently as the 1950s and 1960s and raised in white families. Aboriginal advocates call on the government to offer an apology for these actions and for the subsequent destruction of their culture. Prime Minister Kevin Rudd offered an official apology on February 13, 2008, several months after the writing of this viewpoint. Advocates also call for family support strategies to help break the cycle of cultural disintegration.

As you read, consider the following questions:

1. What did the "Bringing Them Home" report find concerning children who were removed from their homes versus those who grew up with their natural families, according to the author?

2. What catch-22 does Helen Moran mention concerning child safety and culture, according to the viewpoint?

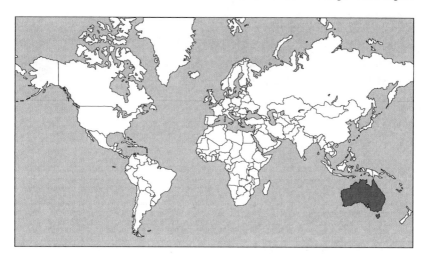

3. According to the viewpoint, who is Neil Harwood and what is his role in the story of the Lost Generations?

Helen Moran's parents knew what was coming.

It was 1960, they had six children and no money, and the NSW [New South Wales] welfare authorities had been looking for them for six months.

Workers eventually tracked the family down just outside Condobolin and Moran, at the age of two, was taken and put into foster care in Sydney, along with her five siblings.

She never saw her parents again and did not even know her father was Aboriginal until she was aged 18 and knocked on her aunt's door in Cobar.

Being part of the Stolen Generations[1] has defined her, but Moran, who says her third and final foster mother was "a wonderful woman", is wary of using hindsight to pass judgment on those who decided to remove her from her parents' care.

---

1. A term used to describe a generation of Australian Aboriginal children taken from their parents and placed with white families.

"We were living in absolute poverty at the time. For me, I look at my life and what I have achieved and been given in life, and I weigh it all up," Moran, who is co-chair of the National Sorry Day[2] Committee, says.

"I think I have been fortunate, a fortunate Stolen Generations person, even though I still have enormous psychological trauma to overcome."

Cultural Genocide

But what she is most critical of is how her case was handled [and] the fact the authorities refused to let her grandmother take care of her and then obstructed her family from contacting the children.

"They covered up our whole Aboriginal identity. . . . I don't have an issue with there being an intervention in my childhood, but to prevent a child having any acknowledgement of their family or extended family, that's when it is cultural genocide."

Advocates argue that, without an official apology from the [Australian] federal government for the removal policies and their consequences, it will be impossible to stop the cycle of destruction and disadvantage still plaguing indigenous Australia.

Moran's experiences, and those of the thousands of children separated from their families from the 1800s until the 1970s, have had a profound impact on generations of indigenous communities and on indigenous and child-protection policy.

Advocates argue that, without an official apology from the federal government for the removal policies and their conse-

---

2. A day specified by the Australian government for apology to the Aboriginal peoples for mistreatment and theft of their children.

quences, it will be impossible to stop the cycle of destruction and disadvantage still plaguing indigenous Australia.

It is a cycle which has come to greater prominence this year as numerous cases of child abuse in indigenous communities have made their way into the media, including one this week [December 2010] of a 10-year-old girl gang raped by nine males in Aurukun, North Queensland.

Two weeks ago, the Darwin Magistrates Court directed two foster carers be tried for manslaughter over the death of a 12-year-old indigenous girl who died lying in the dirt outside their home from a blood infection that could have been easily treated.

In June, the "Little Children Are Sacred" report called for a holistic and integrated approach to systemic sexual abuse of indigenous children, sparking the [Prime Minister John] Howard government's hurried and much criticised Northern Territory intervention.

One in five indigenous children put into foster care had been sexually abused, and one-third of child abuse victims grew up to have difficulties parenting or to abuse their own children.

Many of those now suffering are the children or grandchildren of the Stolen Generations [because] the impact of removal policies is intergenerational.

The Human Rights and Equal Opportunity Commission's inquiry into the Stolen Generations, which resulted in the "Bringing Them Home" report, found those removed as children were twice as likely as those who had grown up with their natural families to use illicit substances or be arrested, and three times as likely to have spent time in jail.

The commission was told that one in five indigenous children put into foster care had been sexually abused, and one-third of child abuse victims grew up to have difficulties parenting or to abuse their own children.

As Moran asks, "If people were not nurtured as children, how can you expect them as adults to provide that which they are still starving for themselves?"

Indigenous Children in Foster Care

Indigenous children are overly represented in child protection statistics across Australia.

The percentage of indigenous children in out-of-home care [is] about 26 per cent of Australian cases [and that figure] has not changed since statistics were first kept in the late 1980s, according to the ACT [Australian Capital Territory] Department of Disability, Housing and Community Services. Of the 399 children in Canberra who have been removed from their homes, 89 are indigenous.

Some argue indigenous children are left in dangerous home situations because child protection workers are too scared to remove them, for fear of creating another stolen generation.

A senior department official with the Queensland Department of Child Safety said this week the 10-year-old girl raped in Aurukun had been returned to her community by officials who did not think it was appropriate she stay in the care of a non-indigenous foster family.

Moran says it is a catch-22; while a child's safety is critical, it is also important they do not lose touch with their culture and identity.

"The ideal situation is for a child to remain with Aboriginal family members or their community, provided they are safe. Quite often, children are removed and put in more dangerous situations. My siblings and I were all exposed to abuse in some form or another.

"There is a lot more conscious awareness now of what is culturally appropriate and the need for children to retain contact with family, so they recognise and value their indigenous identity.

"But there are times when it has got to come down to not that the child is indigenous or not indigenous but that the child is safe."

The director of the Australian National University's Centre for Aboriginal Economic Policy Research, Professor Jon Altman, says determining what action to take over an indigenous child at risk involves a "real moral dilemma".

"In some ways we have a problem that has been created because we have dealt with this same issue so badly in the past. Now we have this legacy of being stolen.

"We do need to be very cautious, but maybe we also need to be a bit more creative, finding other family [to care for a child], or other people to mediate in an appropriate way."

Preventing a Repeat of the Stolen Generations

Maintaining connections is critical to preventing a repeat of the Stolen Generations.

"There is nothing more important for an Aboriginal child than family and kin. . . . But we are clearly seeing a situation where we are having family breakdowns, adults abusing each other, children being abused.

"What we are seeing is a breakdown of tradition resulting in abuse. . . . We have to be realistic about how deeply embedded this problem is."

There is no doubt the lessons learned from the Stolen Generations have affected child protection policy.

Director of Aboriginal and Torres Strait Islander Services with the ACT Department of Disability, Housing and Community Services Neil Harwood says the Royal Commission into Aboriginal Deaths in Custody and the story of the Stolen

Australian Prime Minister Kevin Rudd Says Sorry

I move that today [February 13, 2008] we honour the indigenous peoples of this land, the oldest continuing cultures in human history.

We reflect on their past mistreatment. We reflect in particular on the mistreatment of those who were Stolen Generations—this blemished chapter in our nation's history.

The time has now come for the nation to turn a new page in Australia's history by righting the wrongs of the past and so moving forward with confidence to the future.

We apologise for the laws and policies of successive Parliaments and governments that have inflicted profound grief, suffering and loss on these our fellow Australians. We apologise especially for the removal of Aboriginal and Torres Strait Islander children from their families, their communities and their country.

For the pain, suffering and hurt of these Stolen Generations, their descendants and for their families left behind, we say sorry.

To the mothers and the fathers, the brothers and the sisters, for the breaking up of families and communities, we say sorry.

And for the indignity and degradation thus inflicted on a proud people and a proud culture, we say sorry.

We the Parliament of Australia respectfully request that this apology be received in the spirit in which it is offered as part of the healing of the nation.

Kevin Rudd, "Full Transcript of PM's Speech,"
Australian *(Sydney), February 13, 2008.*

Generations resulted in two "landmark reports that helped inform government policy" on child protection.

His unit was set up in 2005 to address the needs of indigenous children in the ACT and to work on reducing their over-representation in child protection statistics.

But the executive director of the department's Office for Children, Youth and Family Support, Megan Mitchell, stresses that a child deemed at risk will be removed from that situation regardless of their indigenous heritage.

The difference is in what happens after that original decision has been made.

"In the first instance, you try to restore the child to the family unit.

"But then if that's not possible, you'd be looking to the broader extended family or kinship group . . . [then to] a member of the Aboriginal community and . . . [then to] an alternative carer who is culturally competent," Mitchell says. "At the moment, about 70 per cent of children in out-of-home care are with kin or relatives."

The department runs a specific indigenous foster-carer program, which aims to recruit and train families to be carers for indigenous children; all but one of the 14 foster families registered are indigenous.

Child Protection Requires Cultural Sensitivity

The department recognises its work in child protection requires cultural awareness and sensitivity to the experiences of the past. Many indigenous families are wary of "welfare" services and child removal.

Harwood says, "There is a little bit of that [concern], but that is just part of breaking down those barriers. In our area we see that often, but part of the job is to try and build those relationships and [address] perceptions of what was happening in the past. I think we really are on to a new way of doing things now."

Staff are expected and trained to make decisions which are culturally appropriate, and each child is given a cultural care plan to maintain and enhance their identity.

Addressing family and community breakdown starts with an apology and continues with practical measures to address the cycle of disadvantage.

"If you don't have a strong sense of who you are, that affects how you interact with society," Harwood explains.

Mitchell agrees.

"Aboriginal kids deserve the same protection and quality of care as any other child. And if that means having to remove the child, it means doing that, but overlaying that is this deep commitment to ensuring there is connection with family and community, and identity is built.

"It is always a balance. . . . In the end [action] has to be in the best interests of the child."

The department hopes to break the cycle of indigenous disadvantage in the ACT through cross-government programs and through early intervention and family support programs.

For Altman, addressing family and community breakdown and dysfunction starts with an apology and continues with practical measures to address the cycle of disadvantage.

"We have got to get over it as a nation, and say sorry. If we think saying sorry will fix the problem, well clearly it's not going to, but it is a first essential, making people feel better, so there is national recognition.

"My line has been for a long time that we need a symbolic and practical reconciliation. Some of these issues are very difficult and create enormous moral dilemmas, but until we start dealing with the underlying causes of dysfunction, any solution is going to be impractical."

The Promise of an Apology

Prime Minister Kevin Rudd has promised to apologise to the Stolen Generations and Indigenous Affairs Minister Jenny Macklin met this week with the National Sorry Day Committee and other indigenous groups to start the process of formulating an apology.

She said the government recognised the need to incorporate practical measures into any apology and the government would implement a national plan to close the life-expectancy gap between indigenous and non-indigenous Australians.

Moran believes an apology is long overdue, and she welcomes Rudd's promise to offer one. She hopes it is in line with that recommended in the "Bringing Them Home" report, tabled in Parliament 10 years ago [in 1997].

"Whether or not it uses the word sorry, the apology will be empty and meaningless unless the "Bringing Them Home" recommendations are upheld.

"It has to be more than symbolic . . . it needs to acknowledge that this happened and deal with the effects of the policies on 10 generations, on thousands of Aboriginal children."

The Wrongful Adoption of Australian Aboriginal Children Is a Myth

Andrew Bolt

In the following viewpoint, Andrew Bolt argues that the Stolen Generations is a myth, and that it is impossible to find any Aboriginal people who were removed from their homes to be raised by white Australians simply because they were Aborigines. Rather, he says, those children who were removed from their families were taken because their lives were in danger from abuse and neglect. Further, he asserts, Australian law never allowed children to be taken from their homes based solely on their Aboriginal status. Bolt is a Melbourne-based Australian newspaper columnist.

As you read, consider the following questions:

1. Who is the co-chairwoman of the National Sorry Day Committee, as reported by the author?
2. What are the names of six children singled out by advocate Robert Manne as examples of children removed from their homes because of their Aboriginal status, according to the viewpoint?

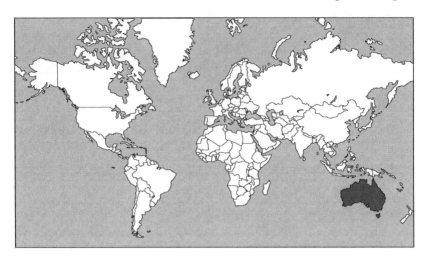

3. According to the viewpoint, who is Doris Kartinyeri?

It's two years [in 2008] since [Australian prime minister] Kevin Rudd said sorry to the "stolen generations[1]", so you'd think someone could have found some of the victims by now.

But no. Last week's [in February 2010] anniversary of the prime minister's speech was marked instead by three efforts which backfired so badly that they merely confirm the "stolen generations" as the greatest lie told of our past.

For years I have publicly challenged the authors of the "stolen generations" myth to name just 10 of the up to 100,000 children they claim were stolen by racist officials simply for being Aboriginal.

To be precise: To name just 10 of the children stolen, as leading propagandist Professor Robert Manne defined it, "not from harm . . . but from their Aboriginality", and by authorities who "wished . . . to help keep White Australia pure".

Just 10. A doddle, right?

---

1. A term used to describe generations of Aboriginal Australians taken from their parents as children and given to white families.

A Failed Challenge

But, strangely, Professor Manne kept failing my challenge. He'd name instead, say, a 12-year-old girl who'd been found with syphilis, or a boy abandoned by his mother, or a boy sent by his mother to a boarding school, or a girl sent to a home by her white father, or a boy rescued from near-slavery, or a boy found by a court to have been neglected by his widowed father, or even children evacuated from war zones in World War II.

And it's the same story again with last week's three Sorry-anniversary attempts at victim-finding.

The most astonishing was that by ABC Radio National's *Awaye!* program, which in a debate about the "stolen generations" presented as a victim Helen Moran, co-chairwoman of the National Sorry Day Committee.

Yet only two years ago, this same ABC had made perfectly clear that Ms Moran was not stolen just for being Aboriginal, but seemed in fact to have been rescued from neglect, if not actual abandonment by her parents, who faced court as a result.

For years I have publicly challenged the authors of the "stolen generations" myth to name just 10 of the up to 100,000 children they claim were stolen by racist officials simply for being Aboriginal.

Ms Moran herself in 2008 explained her removal like this: "We were told different stories so we were told that we were fairly poor, that we were living in bad conditions, we were told that they weren't looking after us properly. We were told that Dad abandoned us all and Mum was left with six children. We were told that we were abandoned by both of them."

Her adoptive mother, Merle Smith, told the same story about Ms Moran's removal from her (actually white) mother: "They never mentioned Aboriginality or anything. Just that the grandmother loved them but couldn't look after them and the reason they were in child care was their mother couldn't cope."

Indeed, Ms Moran was scooped up by welfare officers in Victoria, where, as the Aboriginal-led Stolen Generations Task-force appointed by the [Victoria premier Stephen] Bracks government reported, there had been "no formal policy for removing children from Aboriginal parents".

Conclusion: All the evidence suggests Ms Moran was not stolen, but saved. And if that's true even of the head of the National Sorry Day Committee, how true is it also of the "stolen" people she's meant to represent?

An Example of the Myth

Take, for example, the six "stolen" children presented in the *Age* [Australian newspaper] on Saturday as a "snapshot" of the pain of the "stolen generations". All were siblings of the Edwards family, and included singer Kucha. Again, they were removed in Victoria, which had no law authorising the stealing of children just for being Aboriginal—and other aspects of their case also suggest that's not why they were stolen, either.

Two of their brothers were actually allowed to stay with their parents or relatives, for instance.

And as the *Age* itself reported in 2008, but omitted in Saturday's story, one of the older Edwards children, Arthur, has admitted "phone calls were made to social welfare about Mum not looking after us well".

The siblings deny they were badly cared for, but their welfare—not their Aboriginality—was what had social welfare workers knocking at the door of the family's tin shed.

What's more, the *Age* on Saturday failed to add one more telling detail: that the Edwards children were allowed repeated visits to their mother, by then in Gippsland, apparently without her husband, and that Kucha was returned to her care when he turned 14.

Stolen, yet returned? Doesn't this in fact look like yet another welfare case, with children kept in touch with their dysfunctional families in the hope that one day it will be safe enough for them to go home?

And then came Robert Manne again, this time in the *Monthly*.

In his latest attempt to identify victims, he managed to single out just six children by name: Bob Randall, Doris Kartinyeri, Donna Meehan, Rosalie Fraser, Evelyn Crawford and Ruth Hegarty.

But not one seems to have been stolen "not from harm . . . but from their Aboriginality". Take Randall, the son of white station owner Bill Liddle, who at age seven was sent to the Bungalow at Alice Springs, where he lived while he got a schooling he couldn't get back at the station.

No Government Policy Authorized Stealing Children

He says he was stolen, but the federal court in the Gunner-Cubillo test case found there was no government policy in the Northern Territory then to steal children just for being black.

Nor could it find any example of a child taken for such reasons.

Or take Doris Kartinyeri, of the family behind the Hindmarsh Island "secret women's business" scandal.[2]

She claims she was stolen because her newly widowed father thought he was signing an application for child endowment, rather than for his baby's admission to Colebrook Home.

That excuse alone underlines the fact that South Australian law did not allow children to be stolen just for being Ab-

2. During the 1990s, a political and legal controversy arose in South Australia over the construction of a bridge on land that a group of Aboriginal women claimed was sacred for a secret reason known only to women.

original—as the South Australian Supreme Court indeed found three years ago in the Bruce Trevorrow case.

Were such [Aboriginal] children stolen from loving and caring families—or rescued from neglect, abandonment or harm?

Moreover, the Australian Inland Mission, which ran Colebrook, repeatedly denied stealing children.

And why is Meehan, adopted by a loving white family, on Professor Manne's list? Meehan herself says her mother did not, or could not, say why her children were taken, and in her book she mentions her father only once, only to say she felt no bonding.

Were such children stolen from loving and caring families—or rescued from neglect, abandonment or harm?

You may think the evidence is still too unclear to say.

But when these are the best examples of the "stolen generations", offered to mark the anniversary of Kevin Rudd's sorry, you're entitled to ask if any generation was truly stolen at all.

Canadian First Nations Children Were Wrongfully Taken from Their Families for Adoption

Toronto Star

In the following viewpoint, writers from the Toronto Star *report on a lawsuit filed in Ontario against the Canadian government by Canadian First Nations people who were taken from their families as children. They claim that "the loss of their culture in foster and adoptive care was a wrongful act." The federal government is targeted in the lawsuit because constitutionally the government is responsible for the Native peoples of Canada. Advocates for the indigenous peoples are dismayed that Ottawa is appealing the lawsuit, arguing that such action demonstrates the government's devaluing of Native culture, according to the* Star *writers.*

As you read, consider the following questions:

1. About how many children were taken from aboriginal families during the so-called "Sixties Scoop," according to the viewpoint?

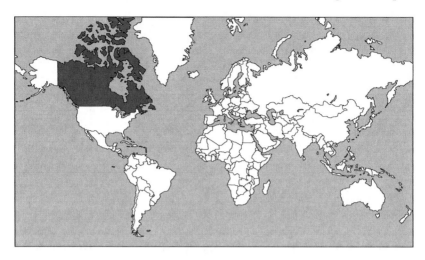

2. When did Rob Lackie finally meet his birth mother, according to the viewpoint?

3. For what did Sheila Fraser criticize Indian Affairs in 2008, according to the viewpoint?

The [Canadian] federal government is fighting a class-action lawsuit by aboriginal children who argue the loss of their culture in foster and adoptive care was a wrongful act—a case that could make Western legal history.

Although Ontario [Association of] Children's Aid agencies took 16,000 children from their families during the so-called Sixties Scoop[1] and placed them in non-aboriginal care, the multimillion-dollar lawsuit names only the attorney general of Canada. Ottawa is constitutionally responsible for Native peoples.

Ottawa quietly appealed the lawsuit in a Toronto courtroom last week [October 28, 2011]—a year after it was certified by the Ontario Superior Court of Justice.

---

1. The Sixties Scoop refers to a Canadian practice that began in the 1960s and continued through the 1980s of placing large numbers of aboriginal children in foster homes or adopting them out to white families.

As a result, the case hasn't gone to court almost three years after it was filed.

Desperate for Roots

Taken as children, the plaintiffs are now middle-aged and, in many cases, desperate to find their roots. They tell stories of abuse, prejudice, loneliness and isolation. They convey a sense of having been treated like commodities rather than human beings. Accounts suggest many were bounced around—even from country to country—with nobody keeping track.

Marcia Brown, 48, is a lead plaintiff on the case. Ontario Children's Aid officials took her from the Beaverhouse First Nation in northeastern Ontario when she was 4.

Brown, who's Ojibwa, went from foster homes to an adoptive home at 9, where she says her non-aboriginal mother tried to wash off her "dirty brown" colour and burned her stuffed tiger full of "Indian bugs."

Taken as children, the plaintiffs are now middle-aged and, in many cases, desperate to find their roots. They tell stories of abuse, prejudice, loneliness and isolation.

After the case was filed in early 2009, she told the *Star*: "I knew God himself didn't want me."

Jeffery Wilson, who represents the aboriginal plaintiffs, criticizes Ottawa for tangling up the suit with legal wrangling paid by taxpayers.

"The attitude of the Crown suggests to my clients that their culture is worth less than nothing," said Wilson, an expert on children and the law. Co-counsel Morris Cooper specializes in class action suits.

Says Cooper: "You're dealing with a defendant (Ottawa) with bottomless resources and certainly no interest in seeing any resolution to this litigation."

From her Kirkland Lake home, Brown says she's disappointed by the appeal. She believes it contradicts public rhetoric about justice for First Nations and Prime Minister Stephen Harper's apology to the aboriginal survivors of residential church schools. The "kill the Indian in the child" mentality of the past is supposed to be defunct.

"It's the same thing," says Brown, of the Sixties Scoop. "I look at this appeal as a lack of respect for our rights and culture. It's just wrong."

When she was 17 and living in Texas with her adoptive mother, the woman took her to the Houston airport, handed her a ticket to Canada and sent her packing with nothing but a suitcase filled with her little girl clothes.

"I didn't get to speak in my own tongue to my grandmother before she passed away," she says. "I didn't fit in anywhere. I saw no difference between myself and a puppy or kitten up for adoption."

"I will never give up. . . . We live in a beautiful country but a great mark—the unpleasant history with the aboriginal people—stains Canada. The Canadian public doesn't know the truth about what happened to the children."

In a 2010 update, Wilson wrote to aboriginal leaders: "For the first time in Western law jurisprudence, a case will proceed on the basis that loss of culture can be litigated as a wrongful act."

Asked why Ottawa is fighting the claims of aboriginal children, an Aboriginal Affairs spokesperson referred the *Star* to the justice ministry. A fax from [the ministry] said it would be "inappropriate" to comment.

"On the matter of costs (of the federal legal team), I will refer you to the department's access to information and privacy office . . . contact information below," the fax says.

Rob Lackie's Story

Rob Lackie, 41, an Inuk from Happy Valley in Labrador, was also part of the Sixties Scoop (which actually ran from 1965 to 1985 with Ontario officials).

Much of his past remains a mystery to him.

It's not clear how Ontario Children's Aid officials were able to offer him for adoption in 1974 to a couple from Georgian Bay. They flew to Newfoundland, picked him up in Bay Bulls and, then back in Ontario, finalized the adoption in Simcoe County.

[Rob Lackie, an Inuk adopted from Newfoundland,] says the biggest loss was growing up without the rich language and culture of his birth. . . . His adoptive parents were kind, but unable to preserve his heritage.

He was 4 and had already been through three foster homes. With two fair, blue-eyed siblings, he realized he was different but didn't know about his Inuit birthright until he was 11.

He didn't meet his biological mother until 2006.

He says the biggest loss was growing up without the rich language and culture of his birth. For that reason, he believes authorities should have focused on finding aboriginal families for the children. Lackie, who lives in Toronto, says: "I always felt as if a big part of my life was missing."

His adoptive parents were kind, but unable to preserve his heritage. He has spent the last few years learning about the Inuit culture and taking classes in the Inuktitut language.

For the first time, too, he met his sister who lives in the U.S. They were separated and he says she doesn't qualify for the class action suit because she's an American citizen.

During the certification hearing in 2010, Wilson cites an exchange with Superior Court Justice Paul Perell. He says Perell inquired what would happen if 16,000 Jews in Canada similarly lost their cultural identity.

Wilson paraphrases his response: "Well, your honour, there would be a huge uproar if 16,000 Jews lost their culture . . . (as there would be) with 16,000 Muslims or 16,000 Hindus." This prompted a clarification that only with First Nations people is there a clear constitutional obligation by the federal government.

A decision on the appeal—before a three-member tribunal that includes Associate Chief Justice J. Douglas Cunningham—is expected this fall.

Since the Toronto case began, similar claims have been launched in B.C. [British Columbia] and Saskatchewan.

The practice of ignoring cultural identity is supposed to be over.

But in her 2008 annual report, then federal auditor Sheila Fraser criticized Indian Affairs for failing to oversee the "cultural appropriateness" of child care services for aboriginal children.

UK Government: Adoption Policy Must Be Colorblind

David Stringer

In the following viewpoint, David Stringer reports on a new British governmental policy calling for a color-blind placement of children in adoptive families. According to Stringer, citing United Kingdom education secretary Michael Gove, race will no longer be an important criterion for adoptive placement. Rather, quickly finding a home for children will be the paramount concern. Stringer notes that black children linger in foster care far longer than do white children. Some social workers, however, suggest that quick placement of black children in white families without appropriate support can be problematic. Stringer is the London correspondent for the Associated Press.

As you read, consider the following questions:

1. About how many children were placed for adoption in the United Kingdom in 2010, according to the viewpoint?

2. Why do black social worker associations in the United States argue that black children should be placed with black adoptive families, as reported by Stringer?

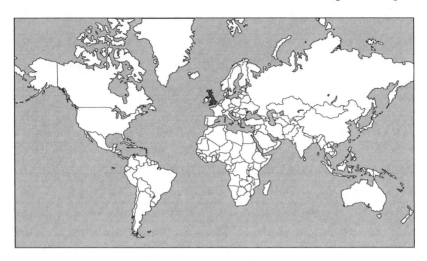

3. According to the author, on average, how long does a white child wait for placement with a permanent adoptive family? How long is the wait for a black or ethnic minority child?

Race should no longer be a key criteria for social workers seeking adoptive families for children in care, Britain's government said Tuesday, stressing that the priority must instead be to find a child a new home quickly.

Education Secretary Michael Gove, who was himself adopted, said that for too long sensitivities about ethnicity had complicated efforts to place black and ethnic minority children, meaning they wait far longer than white children for a permanent home.

Issuing new advice to those working on adoptions, Gove moved Britain closer in line to European neighbors who largely disregard a child's ethnicity.

Dismissing critics which include the National Association of Black Social Workers in the United States, who insist ethnicity must be a concern when matching a child to adoptive parents, he said "politically correct attitudes and ridiculous bureaucracy" had left officials too reluctant to authorize interracial adoptions.

"As a result children from ethnic minority backgrounds languish in care for longer than other kids and are denied the opportunities they deserve," said Gove. "This misguided nonsense punishes those who most need our help and that is why this government is sweeping it away."

He claimed difficulties in placing ethnic minority children who are over-represented in Britain's care system had led to a decline in the country's adoption rate. Figures show 3,200 children were placed for adoption in the U.K. last year, down by about 100 on the previous 12 months.

Will Cooper, a 30-year-old born to an Iranian father and English mother, was adopted by a white English family as an infant. He said his adoptive parents made him aware of his ethnicity, but that it didn't have an impact on his upbringing.

"I really don't think there was any difference to my life. There is that mystery about my background, but it's not something that really affects me," said Cooper, who is running the London Marathon in April to raise money for Action for Children, a charity which helped assist his adoption.

He said Gove was right to challenge the perception that ethnicity should be a factor when deciding whether to place a child with a particular family.

"It should be down to quality of life. If they are the same ethnic background, then great, but it shouldn't be a barrier if they're not," he said.

Social workers have often been reluctant to place children with parents of a different race because of concerns it may make it harder for a child to integrate with the new family, or because it can make it immediately apparent that a child's adoptive parents are not their biological parents.

Some communities have in the past also opposed children being placed with families of a different race, believing adopters should have a detailed understanding of a child's ethnic or religious identity.

In the U.S., the black social workers association and other groups have argued that black children should be placed with black adoptive families if possible, citing the need to preserve links to their ethnic ancestry.

Like Gove, many believe that British adoption officials have long understood their priority to place children with parents of a similar background.

"I do believe there's reluctance among social workers to place kids with families of a different ethnicity, but more due to pressures put upon them by the system," said Cooper.

In both Britain and the U.S., the number of black or ethnic minority children who need adoption is higher than the number of prospective families who share their background. Specific campaigns in the U.K. have attempted to encourage black and other minority families to put themselves forward as prospective adopters.

Britain's new advice orders social workers to make placing a child with any suitable family their priority. Gove said speed must trump concerns over "skin color, or faith, or ethnic background."

The education ministry said that on average, a white child waits 610 days to be placed with a permanent adoptive family, while black and ethnic minority children wait about 966 days—almost a full year longer.

"I know that children tend to do well when placed with a family who shares their ethnic or cultural background, but I know also that delay can have a very detrimental effect," said children's minister Tim Loughton.

"If there can be an ethnic match that's an advantage, possibly a very significant one. But, it should never be a dealbreaker," he said.

Judith Washington, a retired social worker who spent 15 years handling adoptions in New York, said pressure to find

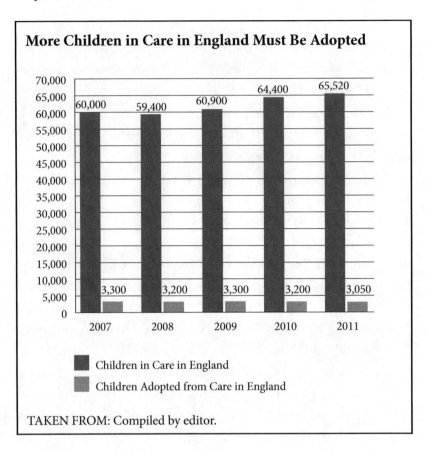

More Children in Care in England Must Be Adopted

Children in Care in England
Children Adopted from Care in England

TAKEN FROM: Compiled by editor.

children a permanent adoptive family quickly can lead to mistakes or a lack of vital preparation work.

> *The education ministry said that on average, a white child waits 610 days to be placed with a permanent adoptive family, while black and ethnic minority children wait about 966 days—almost a full year longer.*

"People who adopt also need help to understand the implications, and to optimize the chances of the adoption being a success," said Washington, who retired in 2004.

She said it's vital those adopting a child of another race have the right support before the child joins their family.

Washington said there had been little research to examine the success of adoptions where children are placed with parents of another race.

Gove said his own experience meant it was a personal crusade to increase the numbers of children in public care who are placed with new families.

"I was given a second chance and as a result of the love and affection, the stability and care that my parents gave me, all the opportunities that I subsequently had in life were there," he said.

Jesse Washington in Philadelphia, David Crary in New York, Jan Olsen in Copenhagen, Barry Hatton in Lisbon, Jorge Sainz in Madrid and Louise Nordstrom in Stockholm contributed to this report.

Children Should Be Placed in Same-Race Families

Joseph Harker

In the following viewpoint, Joseph Harker argues that the new British policy of downplaying race in adoption placements is wrong. While he agrees that finding a stable home for children is of utmost importance, he also believes that accounting for race remains an important value to help children stay connected to their cultural roots. He argues that it is important for a black or Asian adoptee to have a parent who shares firsthand the experience of being a member of a minority race. Harker is a black British journalist.

As you read, consider the following questions:

1. How many children are in foster care, according to Harker? Of these, what percentage are members of racial minorities?

2. What does Harker say about his own upbringing as the son of an Irish mother and Nigerian father who left before he was born, and subsequent adoption by his white stepfather?

3. According to Harker, what does the "mainstream political agenda" say migrants and minorities must do to be accepted in Britain?

Joseph Harker, "Comment: This Rush to Downplay Race Ignores the Truth of Adoption," *Guardian* (London), November 3, 2010, p. 30. Copyright © 2010 by the Guardian. All rights reserved. Reproduced by permission.

According to the children's minister [of the United Kingdom], there is "no reason at all" why white couples should not adopt black or Asian children. Instinctively, many people would agree with Tim Loughton when he says: "If it is a great couple offering a good, loving, stable permanent home, that should be the number one consideration." After all, isn't being in a loving, caring home all that counts?

Well, ideally, yes. But as a black person adopted as a child by a white parent I believe this notion is simplistic. There are about 65,000 children in care at present, 20% of whom are from racial minorities. Approximately 2,300 were approved for adoption last year [2009], of whom 500 were of black or Asian origin.

There has long been a shortage of black or Asian families willing to adopt, so in the 1960s and '70s it was common for white parents to be approved to raise minority children. At the time, little attention was paid to the child's cultural needs, and many grew up feeling disconnected from their racial background.

As a result, black campaigners successfully changed adoption procedures so that the default position was for black children to be adopted by black parents. This would have worked well, but in practice the shortage of black would-be adopters left many children languishing in care for years. No one would now say this was acceptable, and in 1998 the then education minister Paul Boateng—whose wife Janet had been prominent in the same-race campaign two decades earlier—relaxed the rules to make it easier for transracial adoptions to take place. "The importance of family life to a child cannot be overstated," he said.

Race Is Being Downplayed

Since then, for the most part, though race has been an important factor, individual decisions have sought a balance in the best interests of the child. Loughton's comments, however, appear to tip this balance so that race is at risk of being down-played altogether. His priorities seem to be finding a nice family and placing the child quickly. Presumably well-spoken middle-class types will be at the front of every queue.

My own Nigerian father abandoned my Irish mother before I was born. Three years later she married an English local, who later adopted me, and I took his name. I was never short of love, support and encouragement. But when race regularly collided with my life I was ill-prepared. I found it difficult to cope with the playground and classroom taunts and, as I grew older, the disconnect with my African heritage became more of an issue. I've spoken to many black people of similar upbringing and they often talk of the same experiences.

The media often likes to talk to children about how they feel about being transracially adopted. Every time I hear these reports I know they are asking the wrong people—because it is only in later life that one can appreciate what has been missed.

The stridency of Loughton's words gives me little faith that he understands these issues. Moreover, his thinking entirely fits a mainstream political agenda running for most of the past decade, which scorns multiculturalism and tries to deny difference. An agenda which says that in order to be accepted in Britain, migrants and minorities must speak the language fluently, adopt "British values" (whatever they are) and ditch their religious beliefs: to assimilate into this country rather than maintain their cultural traditions and historical ties.

On Monday [November 1, 2010], paradoxically, an elderly black couple went to court to claim that they'd been denied the chance to become foster carers because of their Christian-based views on homosexuality. They didn't believe it was an acceptable lifestyle. Clearly these views are outdated, but the fact remains that they are held by many who originate from strongly religious countries in the Caribbean, Africa and Asia. So, if the couple's claims are correct, would the adoption rules now in effect state that black and Asian children can no longer be adopted by those who share their cultural heritage? If so, combined with the message Loughton is sending out, we could be moving towards an effective whites-only adoption policy.

Yes, stable homes are always better than living in care. But to deny the importance of race is not only insulting to minorities, it also risks causing unnecessary confusion and distress to . . . vulnerable children.

Race Will Always Be a Factor

There was a time when politicians claimed to welcome difference, declaring that it strengthened Britain by connecting our country to the rest of the world. Now it seems the government believes that black or Asian families have little to offer children from their own background. The common heritage is either irrelevant, undesirable, or something so meaningless that a white parent who's visited their local library's diversity section could do just as well.

The fact is, race will always be a factor in a black or Asian child's life, and having a parent who understands this through their own direct life experience is a huge benefit. Indeed, one needn't get too hung up on whether the parents precisely match the racial makeup of the child, which can often be complex. Whether the couple is black, mixed or Asian, they'll almost certainly understand the importance of a nonwhite child's cultural needs.

Yes, stable homes are always better than living in care. But to deny the importance of race is not only insulting to minorities, it also risks causing unnecessary confusion and distress to those vulnerable children who look to the state to protect them.

Periodical Bibliography

The following articles have been selected to supplement the diverse views presented in this chapter.

Barbara Amiel — "When This Baby Finds Out Later," *Maclean's*, vol. 122, no. 8, October 5, 2009.

Nicole Baute — "'Are You OK?': Transracial Adoption Is Increasingly Popular but That Doesn't Mean It's Easy for Children or Their Families," *Toronto Star*, March 13, 2010.

David M. Brodzinsky, Charlotte J. Patterson, and Mahnoush Vaziri — "Adoption Agency Perspectives on Lesbian and Gay Prospective Parents: A National Study," *Adoption Quarterly*, vol. 5, no. 3, March 2002.

Julie Griffiths — "We Can't Go for an Ethnic Match at Any Price," *Community Care*, March 3, 2011.

Dan Harrison — "Call for Nation to Apologise over Forced Adoptions," *Sydney Morning Herald*, March 1, 2012.

Sharon Jayson — "US Adoption Is Increasingly Crossing Racial and Ethnic Lines; But 'Colorblind' Childrearing May Not Be the Way to Go," *USA Today*, April 11, 2011.

Emma Macdonald — "Apology Won't Heal Adoption Wounds," *Canberra Times* (Australia), February 29, 2012.

Hannah Martin — "A Family Reaches Out for Help," *Sunday Tasmanian* (Australia), August 28, 2011.

Lindsay Murdoch — "Fate of East Timor's Stolen Generation in Indonesia Finally Comes to Light," *Sydney Morning Herald*, March 5, 2012.

Peter Stanford — "Are We Doing Our Best for Children in Care?," *Daily Telegraph*, September 30, 2011.

GLOBALVIEWPOINTS

The Rights of Adoptive Parents, Birth Parents, and Adoptees

In the United States, Adoptees Fight to Have Their Birth Records Unsealed

Joyce Bahr

In the following viewpoint, Joyce Bahr argues that adoptees should have the right to their birth certificates. She asserts that the National Council for Adoption's ongoing stand against legislation that would open adoption records demonstrates its focus on denying rights to adoptees and birth parents. In addition, she argues that it has been demonstrated that neither adoptees nor birth mothers have privacy rights. Since this is the case, she concludes, adoptees should be the ones to choose whether they want to have their original birth certificate. Bahr is a mother who surrendered her child for adoption in 1966.

As you read, consider the following questions:

1. In what states did the National Council for Adoption (NCFA) lobby against open records bills, according to the author?

2. What percentage of NCFA members are affiliated with either the Church of Jesus Christ of Latter-Day Saints or Bethany Christian Services, according to Bahr?

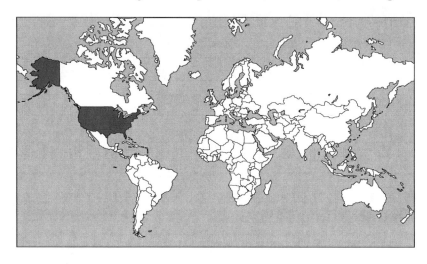

3. According to the viewpoint, what did the Donaldson report recommend for every state's laws in November of 2007?

The National Council for Adoption [NCFA] formed in 1980 after England unsealed birth certificates in 1975 and a federal class action lawsuit by 19 members of the New York chapter of the Adoptees' Liberty Movement Association was defeated, because a Texas Republican senator and adoptive parent used his power to do so. Also at this time, adoption social workers were communicating with the U.S. Department of Health, Education, and Welfare [HEW] about reforming adoption, and HEW wanted to open records for adoptees and birth parents throughout the country.

There is speculation the NCFA was formed not only to promote adoption but to prevent adoptee and birth parent rights, and this they have done. Not only did they lobby against the Tennessee and Oregon open records bills, they also legally challenged the new laws. However, they were unsuccessful in court challenges to the Tennessee Supreme Court, the U.S. Court of Appeals to the Sixth Circuit and the Oregon Appellate Court, as they were unable to produce even one written promise of confidentiality. Also they were unable to prove unsealing birth certificates would cause more abortions.

During the Tennessee initiative to open records, only one agency in the state, the Small World Adoption Agency operated by the Mormon Church, joined the NCFA to lobby against the bill while other adoption agencies in the state spoke out, saying the NCFA does not want to reform adoption.

Characterizing the NCFA

The NCFA is a Washington, DC-based trade association with 184 private agency members, of which 61% are either [Church of Jesus Christ of] Latter-Day Saints [Mormons] or Bethany Christian Services affiliated. They advocate for confidential adoption and deny that adoptees have the need for contact and information about birth families. They fail to recognize grief issues for adoptees and for mothers who surrendered to adoption. For many years, they have said the few adoptees who search [for their birth parents] are degenerates and misfits. The thousands of birth/natural mothers who have searched are not mentioned at all. Instead of any concern for mothers and acknowledgement of the injustice of forced adoptions, they continue their lies of privacy rights.

Surrendering mothers like myself signed surrender papers terminating parental rights for the purpose of adoption placement, and these papers state nothing about confidentiality or a privacy right afforded mothers. When abortion was legalized in 1973, women were given a legal right to privacy in the early trimester of abortion, but there was never any right given to mothers who surrendered, and adoption agencies never gave us a document signed by them stating we would have confidentiality. Certainly agencies could never give anyone a right and they had no intention of giving a mother legal confidentiality. No options to keep your baby were presented and most mothers were manipulated and coerced in a surrender process all about signing the baby away.

Some social workers made statements indicating a surrendering mother would have confidentiality, but what did it mean? Was it legally binding, when courts have held that adoption professionals' verbal statements of confidentiality cannot be permitted to tie the hands of legislatures? No, neither a social more nor a verbal statement are legally binding [nor are they] supported in a statute. For some, the word confidentiality was heard because the agency wanted to let you know they had no intention of telling anyone you were pregnant out of wedlock, but they were not saying they could somehow prevent your child from one day finding you. Nor could they prevent social mores from changing. It was confidential; however, no confidentiality was given.

Did mothers ask for confidentiality? No, it was imposed on some of them and in private adoptions attorneys never mentioned it. Pregnant mothers were being told what to do and doomed to lose their child because they were unmarried.

It should be the adult adoptee's decision to seek the answer to their identity and be able to request a copy of their birth certificate if they so choose.

Research by the Evan B. Donaldson Adoption Institute, the foremost think tank on adoption issues, in its study "For the Records, Restoring a Legal Right for Adult Adoptees," finds there is no constitutional right to prevent the disclosure of "confidential" information. Courts have held that the constitutional right of privacy has never included a general right to the nondisclosure of all forms of information that an individual may prefer to keep secret.

The Reformed Church of America Supports Adoptee Rights

It is recommended at the national level to promote policy changes regarding state laws on two aspects that affect adult adoptees. It is important for each state to amend its laws to restore unrestricted access for adult adoptees to their original birth certificates. Then it is recommended that at the national policy level, the appropriate child welfare agencies build on the experiences of the states that have restored the access of adult adoptees. Further, it is timely for educational institutions, as well as the appropriate federal and state child welfare agencies, to conduct social science research. Such research would be important to expand the understanding of the experiences of adopted persons, birth parents, and adoptive parents in relationship to the access-of-records issue. Lastly, educational institutions and churches should be encouraged to provide accurate data on adoption issues in order to counter myths and misinformation about the issues surrounding adoption legislation and concepts. Churches would be the most likely institutions to disseminate information on the spiritual issues affecting adoptees, birth parents, and adoptive parents.

Reformed Church of America, "The Medical, Psychological and Spiritual Health of Persons Who Are Adopted," Report to Congregations and Assemblies from the 2010 Synod, *2010.*

No Justification for Denying Adoptees Birth Certificates

Most Americans support adoptees and birth parents in their searches and many do search, however, if there were a right to privacy for birth parents or adoptees it could have put a damper on searching a long time ago. So there are no privacy rights for birth mothers or fathers and there is no justification for denying adoptees the inalienable right to a copy of their own birth certificate. Mutual consent registries do not work for all and give many no other recourse than to search.

The NCFA should not speak for the thousands of adult adoptees who want to quit wondering, have questions answered, and who realize the importance of knowing their identity for [reasons of] health and well-being. It should be the adult adoptees' decision to seek the answer to their identity and be able to request a copy of their birth certificate if they so choose. The Donaldson report released in November of 2007 did not rely on disapproved assumptions and the misrepresentation of statistical data as the NCFA would like people to believe. The report recommends for every state's laws to restore unrestricted access for adult adopted persons to their original birth certificate and it acknowledges the fundamental right to know.

Unsealing Adoption Records in New Jersey Will Do More Good than Harm

Elizabeth S. Cole

In the following viewpoint, legal expert Elizabeth S. Cole presents an argument for the unsealing of adoptee birth records in the state of New Jersey. She first dismantles the misrepresentation that adoptions must be kept confidential for the sake of the birth mother. She notes that most adoptions are among people who already know each other and are thus not confidential. In addition, most birth parents would welcome contact from their children. Secondly, she demonstrates that abortions do not increase as a result of open birth records. Finally, she asserts that it is "true and fair" to help adoptees find their roots.

As you read, consider the following questions:

1. According to the author, in what year was the highest number of adoptions recorded in the United States? How many adoptions occurred in that year?
2. What percentage of all US unrelated adoptions in 2006 was of infants, according to the viewpoint?
3. What did a New Jersey law require a birth parent to do before 1993, as reported by the author?

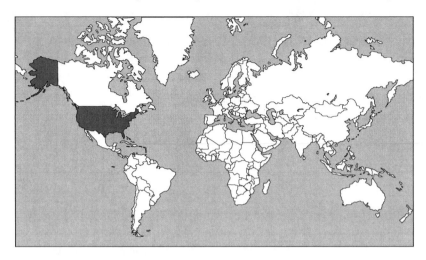

For over twenty-seven years [since 1980], legislation has been regularly introduced in New Jersey that would make it possible for adults who have been adopted to obtain a copy of their original birth certificate. They would have the same right as anyone who was not adopted, simply by going to the Office of Vital Statistics and Registry and requesting it. S1087, which has passed the Senate, would authorize access. It has a provision to allow birth parents from the past to have their name deleted from the birth certificate that would be released to the adopted person. It also provides all birth parents, past and future, to indicate their preference regarding contact.

I believe that a similar bill has not been passed in the Assembly because those opposed have prevailed by insisting that the legislation be more complicated and costly than it need be. Twenty-seven years ago, they argued that the negative effects of the legislation would be worse than the good it might do. Some of their hypotheses were reasonable then given that there was little experience with similar bills. Now with eight states having legislation to allow adopted adults access to their original birth records, these hypotheses have been tested. What have we learned? Even with data that contradicts and disproves their contentions, the opposition in New Jersey has not changed its position. Opinion thrives without the nutriment of fact.

Legislators Did Not Receive Full Information

Based on my conversations and reading of past testimony, I have concluded that some vital information needed to make an informed decision was not received by legislators, and that they may have also been given misinformation on critical issues.

These are the most serious of the misrepresentations:

1. This legislation will affect most of the past, current and future adoptions in New Jersey since they were and are confidential or closed.

2. If records are unsealed, women who once would have chosen confidential adoption might choose abortion instead.

3. Contact from adoptees is unwelcome by birth parents.

The Statistics of Confidential Adoption

1. *How many adoptions can be considered confidential?*

No good statistical information exists nationwide or in New Jersey which would give the exact number of adoptions that would be affected by this legislation. What we do know is that in 1944 estimated adoptions in all of the United States for that year were 50,000. The highest number was 175,000 in 1970. Since the 1970s, the stigma attached to unmarried parenthood reduced dramatically. Unwed mothers were no longer expelled from school, shunned by their friends or considered pariahs or outcasts. Popular culture began to celebrate the single parenthood of celebrities. For some women keeping their children became a real choice that their older sisters never had. Consequently the numbers of babies placed for adoption fell. In 1973, 8.7 percent of never-married women placed their children for adoption. By 1995, that number had dropped to only 0.9 percent.

Since 1987, the number of adoptions in the United States has remained constant from 118,000 to 127,000. For the last twenty-seven years, the growth in adoptions within this group has been in placements by public agencies and in intercountry adoptions. Infant domestic adoption rates have been falling since 1970.

However, many in the general public, including legislators, believe that since 1940 when records were sealed, the majority, if not all adoptions nationwide and in New Jersey, have been of infants. Further, they believe they were "closed" or "traditional" unrelated infant adoptions—those where the identity of the birth and adoptive parents are not known to each other and where no contact after the adoption is anticipated. Understanding the scope of the population affected is critical in decision making.

Since the 1970s, the stigma attached to unmarried parenthood reduced dramatically.

Most Adoptions Are Not Confidential

From 1951 to 1996, fifty one percent (51%) of all adoptions were not confidential because they consisted mostly of stepparents adopting their spouses' children or of people adopting their relatives. The proportion of relative adoptions is predicted to remain high. Not only are the parties' identities known to each other, they are living together.

Not all of the remaining unrelated adoptions can be considered confidential.

Children are placed with adoptive parents by public or private agencies or independent of agencies by private individuals (doctors, lawyers, ministers, etc.).

Nationwide, adoptions by public agencies began to increase in the late sixties and early seventies. As infants became less available for adoption, they placed children from foster care who were older or who had special needs. Public agency placements were 18 percent of all adoptions in 1987, and they have risen, in 2001 to 40 percent and to 56 percent in 2006. In New Jersey, they accounted for 43 percent of all adoptions in 2001. The increase from the late sixties on is due to the availability of adoption subsidies, more frequent case reviews and a refocusing of services to children with special needs.

The majority of adoptions made by public agencies after 1968 should not be considered confidential, because they were of foster parents adopting their foster children or of older children who know their identities.

In 1998, 65 percent of all public agency adoptions were foster parent adoptions. Foster parents know the children's last names, and where they were from, and they may have even had a relationship with the birth parents. Older children being prepared for placement with adoptive parents are generally given information on who they were, how they came to be in foster care and why they cannot be with their birth parents.

Some Adoptions Are Confidential

The majority of private agency adoptions from 1945 to 1970 can be considered confidential. Since 1970, the total number of infant adoptions began a steady decline. One 2006 estimate places them at only 9 to 10 percent of all U.S. unrelated adoptions. A growing number of them are either "open" adoptions or "mediated" adoptions—where birth parents choose the adoptive parents, whom they actually meet and with whom they may continue contact. Thirty-one percent of current private agency placements in New Jersey are of children from other countries. We can conclude that current and future private agency adoptions will be the smallest segment of all adoptions.

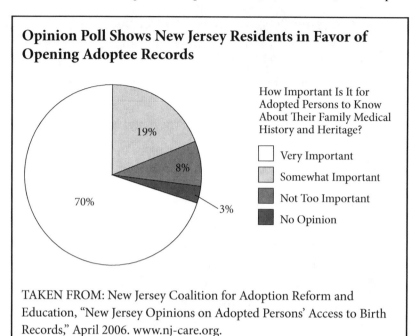

Opinion Poll Shows New Jersey Residents in Favor of Opening Adoptee Records

How Important Is It for Adopted Persons to Know About Their Family Medical History and Heritage?

☐ Very Important

▨ Somewhat Important

▩ Not Too Important

■ No Opinion

19%

8%

70%

3%

TAKEN FROM: New Jersey Coalition for Adoption Reform and Education, "New Jersey Opinions on Adopted Persons' Access to Birth Records," April 2006. www.nj-care.org.

It is usual in intercountry adoptions for the adoptive parents to know the last name of the child they adopt. Since many have gone to the country of origin, they know the name of the orphanage or agency through which their child was placed. It is possible, but highly improbable, that these adoptees will have contact with their birth parents of origin, if and when they have access to their original birth records.

The Trend Toward Open Adoption

Not all independent adoptions are closed.

The number of adoptions done independently of agencies has fluctuated over the years. In 1992 in New Jersey, they accounted for 17 percent (363 of 2,083) of total adoptions. In 1993, they were 158 of 1,300 adoptions or 12 percent, and in 1994, they were 195 of 1,138 (17 percent). Before 1993, New Jersey law required that a birth parent in an independent adoption must directly place the child in the hands of the adoptive parents. Intermediaries were not allowed because birth parents were to have made an informed consent to the adoption by having firsthand knowledge of the people with whom they were making the placement. It was also done to stop the possibility that an intermediary could have stolen the child from its birth parents.

Since 1993, New Jersey has made legal the use of non-agency intermediaries. In every case, the adoption had to go to court to be finalized, and an agency was appointed to make an Adoption Complaint Investigation (ACI). Little is known about how "open" or "closed" these placements are because no data is collected. There is some anecdotal information, however. I recently spoke with experienced social workers that have performed these investigations over the years. They indicate that, while most were, not all of these adoptions were confidential. Adoptive parents in many instances have known the last name of the birth parents—some have documents with that information on them. Some adoptive parents have even been present at the child's birth. The social workers also felt, based on their experience, that there was a trend to more openness in independent adoption overall.

Allowing adopted adults access to their original birth records will affect a much smaller population than is generally believed and that group is expected to be even smaller in the future.

2. *Have women chosen abortion rather than adoption in those states where adoption records have been unsealed?*

Twenty-seven years ago, several groups testifying against the New Jersey legislation to allow adoptees access to their original birth records expressed the not unreasonable fear that allowing access might lead to more birth mothers choosing abortion rather than adoption. Since that time, this hypothesis has been tested and not supported. *There is no evidence that abortions have increased in those jurisdictions having access.*

There is contrary evidence that adoptions have increased in these states. I am at a loss to understand why this allegation continues to be offered and accepted as valid objection to the current proposed legislation.

3. What has been the reaction of New Jersey birth parents who have been asked if they would like to have contact with the child they placed for adoption?

The basic objection to giving adopted adults a copy of their original birth certificate is that they would use it to find their birth parents. The groups opposing the legislation allege that such contact would be unwelcome and damaging. They believe the alleged promise of confidentiality creates a shield against this unwelcome contact and should stay in place. This hypothesis might have been reasonable twenty-seven years ago, but is no longer defensible. Experience in New Jersey shows that they are protecting people who want to be found. For twenty years, the Division of Youth and Family Services has been contacting birth parents whose adopted children are searching for them. They have consistently reported that 95 percent of all birth parents desire contact.

The Law Should Be Changed

Confidential adoptions have always been the smallest segment of all New Jersey adoption. Beginning in 1970, they began to decline nationally until, at the present time, they should be thought of as less than 10 percent of all adoptions. Allowing adopted adults access to their original birth records will affect a much smaller population than is generally believed and that group is expected to be even smaller in the future. Once more, most birth parents will continue to welcome contact. Any legislation to protect the small number of birth parents who wish confidentiality should not be so costly and cumbersome that it deters adopted adults from obtaining their original birth certificates.

Finally, I was dismayed to see the list of organizations that oppose this legislation in New Jersey. Some have not changed their position in twenty-seven years, although our experience and research show it is untenable. National standard-setting bodies such as the Child Welfare League [of America] and the National Association of Social Workers are in favor of providing adoptees access to their records. I am puzzled as to why the opposition maintains their stance. Are they unaware of the evidence? Do they continue to hold to beliefs without the nutriment of fact? If either of these positions is true, what compromises can they bring to the table in forming a law that is fair, informed and relevant to those whose lives it affects? It is my hope that New Jersey legislators are not blinded by the list of impressive opposing organizations and look beyond them to what is true and fair. This is what the legislature did when it took on gun control and civil unions. I hope they do for adoptees seeking their roots what they have done on these other issues—the right thing—no matter what organization was offended.

Adoptees Return to Korea to Argue for the Rights of Birth Parents and Adoptees

Shannon Heit

In the following viewpoint, Shannon Heit reports on the effort to change adoption laws in Korea, led by Korean adoptees who have returned to their homeland. The group believes that if there were more governmental support and financial assistance to single mothers, far fewer children would be offered up for international adoption. They also argue that adoption agencies have used unethical practices in the past, and this is one reason the agencies lobby for closed adoption records. Finally, she notes, many feel it is a priority that Korean children should be raised in Korea. Heit is a journalist and a returning Korean adoptee.

As you read, consider the following questions:

1. How many Korean children have been adopted abroad since 1958, according to Heit?
2. What percentage of Korean children given up for adoption are children of single mothers, according to the viewpoint?
3. As reported by the author, what does Professor David Smolin call the falsification of records to facilitate adoption?

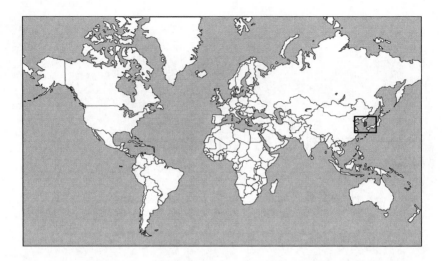

everaging the help of a group of lawyers and a Korean unwed mothers' organization, a group of Koreans adopted
abroad are driving a movement to create a major shift in how
the country deals with adoptions.

With the support of Democratic Party Representative Choi
Young-hee, this coalition presented its bill to revise the current Special Act Relating to Adoption Promotion and Procedure law at a National Assembly public hearing on Nov. 10
[2009].

The coalition has been working together for over a year to
draw up a proposal for a new adoption law. Involved are three
adoption-related groups—Truth and Reconciliation for the
Adoption Community of Korea (TRACK), Adoptee Solidarity
Korea [ASK], KoRoot—an unwed mothers' group, Korean Unwed Mothers' Families Association (KUMFA), and the Gong-
gam Korean Public Interest Lawyers' Group.

Changing the Course of Korea's Adoption Laws

What initially began last year [2008] as a request to the Anti-
Corruption and Civil Rights Commission for a probe into
cases of allegedly inaccurate or falsified adoption records has

expanded into a movement that could change the course of Korea's adoption program.

So Ra Mi, the Gong-gam lawyers' group representative, said that while the probe failed to "correct the wrongdoings of the past," she wanted to "help change the present and future" of Korean adoption.

Korea has a long history of international adoption. According to the Ministry of Health and Welfare, since 1958 over 160,000 children have been sent abroad for adoption. Other estimates put the figure closer to 200,000, due to the many unrecorded adoptions performed in the years before 1958. Intercountry adoption began in Korea during the 1950s after the Korean War, initiated as an effort to help children orphaned by the war and children born to Korean mothers and U.N. [United Nations] coalition fathers.

The adoption program, however, quickly became what critics now say has been a substitute for any real government-level social welfare programs for children.

Adoption rates steadily grew throughout the 1980s, long after war orphans ceased needing homes. It wasn't until the 1988 Olympics in Korea that adoption rates fell, due to a wave of international media dubbing Korea a "baby exporting nation." This stigmatized reputation still holds today, as does Korea's intercountry adoption program that last year sent more than 1,000 children overseas.

Intercountry adoption began in Korea during the 1950s after the Korean War, initiated as an effort to help children orphaned by the war and children born to Korean mothers and [United Nations] coalition fathers.

Now those who were adopted abroad have returned to change the very program that sent them away.

Although Korea ranks as the fifth-largest "sending" country of international adoption—behind China, Guatemala, Russia, and Ethiopia—it has never ratified the Hague Convention on [Protection of Children and Co-operation in Respect of] Intercountry Adoption, nor does it meet the international standards of the U.N. Convention on the Rights of the Child.

The government has been maneuvering in what seems like steps [addressing] the issue. In recent years, task forces were created to research and propose revisions to adoption laws. But critics point out that these government task forces didn't originally include any adoptee organizations or single mothers' groups, the groups that would be intimately affected by such changes.

TRACK president Jane Jeong Trenka believes that these groups are a valuable voice in the discussion. "It is significant that our bill has been written by a coalition of concerned Korean citizens and diasporic Koreans, international adoptees, and single Korean mothers who will reap absolutely no economic, professional, or social benefit from continuing the adoption system as it has been practiced in the past. Instead, we look forward to meeting international standards of human rights and justice," said Trenka.

Preserving and Supporting Families

One of the biggest differences in the new bill that the coalition hopes to make into law is taking the focus away from promoting adoption. Instead, more emphasis would be placed on the preservation and support of original families.

According to Ministry of Health and Welfare statistics on adoption, 90 percent of children who are adopted, both internationally and domestically, are children of single mothers. This is indicative of the strong social stigma that unwed mothers face, as well as the lack of financial support from the government should they choose to keep their children.

Currently, single mothers who apply for government assistance can receive only 50,000 won per month ($43), based on whether or not they meet low-income stipulations. During the open floor portion of this week's [in November 2009] public hearing, a member from the unwed mothers' group KUMFA questioned the seemingly preferential treatment for adoptive families over single mothers. She raised the point that families who adopt domestically within Korea are able to receive 100,000 won per month in government assistance, with no low-income stipulations, versus the 50,000 won that is provided to unwed mothers.

The discrepancy points to a clear case of institutionalized discrimination against unwed mothers, says the group.

The central government's concern over the plummeting birthrate, and its policies on adoption and social spending for women and children, seems contradictory. Because Korea's birthrate is the lowest of all Organisation for Economic Cooperation and Development countries, the government has taken great strides to promote an increase in the birthrate; there are government incentives for families with multiple children, supporting child care, and education subsidies.

There is a general consensus that giving more adequate support to single mothers would go a long way in both stemming the country's low birthrate and creating a more ethical environment in adoption procedures.

The Government Should Help Single Mothers

Skeptics say it seems counterproductive, then, that the government is doing little to keep children already here, born to single mothers, in the country. When interviewed about her reasons for spearheading the adoptee coalition's bill, Rep. Choi explained that more needs to be done to support unwed mothers.

"The government is urging people to have children, but on the other hand, isn't supporting the children of unwed

183

South Korea Changes Adoption Laws

Over the almost 60 years of South Korea's adoption history, 220,000 adopted and forgotten children equal 220,000 birth mothers equal 220,000 families separated by deeply rooted discrimination, not always by choice.

By making the new adoption bill law, South Korea can begin reconciling its painful adoption past by changing its current systematic placement of Korean children through the erasure of their identities and coercion of their mothers. In this way, South Korea can work to set new precedents in adoption justice.

Jennifer Kwon Dobbs,
"Ending South Korea's Child Export Shame,"
Foreign Policy in Focus, June 23, 2011. www.fpif.org.

---

mothers. . . . It shouldn't just be about encouraging more babies but to also raise well the babies already born. . . . The most important thing is these babies are not just the children of single mothers, but they are all of our children," she said.

There is a general consensus that giving more adequate support to single mothers would go a long way in both stemming the country's low birthrate and creating a more ethical environment in adoption procedures.

Choi Hyoung-sook, a representative from KUMFA, spoke during the hearing and gave examples of policies in other advanced countries, such as France, Sweden, Germany and the United States, that have increased the birthrate and helped single mothers keep their children. "In reality, unwed mothers are forced to choose adoption, for lack of another option. Therefore, I think there should be policy measures created to support single mothers," she said.

Her thoughts were echoed by Yang Jung-ja, director of the Korea Family Legal Service Center. Yang spoke [about] France's success in increasing their birthrate though government support for single mothers or unmarried couples. "In the past, France had the lowest birthrate in the world, but now it has the highest rate in Europe ... 52 percent of its children are born out of wedlock but they still get government support."

KUMFA representative Choi Hyoung-sook also indicated a need for government-sponsored counseling for single mothers during and after their pregnancies. "Adoption agencies pressure you to give up your child. . . . They don't offer counseling on how to raise your child. . . . I believe that the goal is to get the mother to give up the baby.

"(Adoption) agencies should not be the first and only ones to provide counseling; there should be a neutral government agency," Choi Hyoung-sook said.

Red Flags Raised

These cases bring up obvious red flags over the questionable ties between unwed mothers' homes and adoption agencies. All four of the major adoption agencies in Korea operate their own unwed mothers' homes, a practice critics have labeled "baby farming."

Choi Hyoung-sook said she was pressured to relinquish her son for adoption within six hours of giving birth. She later retracted her decision to relinquish and had to go through great measures to get her son back. Other mothers like her, she recounted, were forced to pay fees to the agencies for each day that the child stayed in their facilities in order to get their children back.

Choi Hyoung-sook says it's not right that agencies ask mothers to make a decision about adoption so soon after giving birth. "This is not a time when a mother is able to make an informed decision."

In Korea, there are currently no regulations on the timeline of a mother's consent to adoption. The coalition's revisions would include a stipulation that consent from a mother is not valid until 30 days after the birth of the child, giving the mother ample time to get counseling about parenting resources and to understand all of the implications of such a weighty decision. It also would include an extension on the time period that mothers are able to retract their decision.

Bringing the time period to 30 days would bring Korea up to international standards.

The Need for National Regulations

International adoption standards aside, there is also a lack of clear national regulations, which can create questions of ethics in adoption agencies' procedures. Adoption agencies here run essentially as private organizations with little to no interference from the government. It is a troubling fact, given that their line of work deals with the welfare of the country's most vulnerable citizens—children.

According to the new bill, agencies would be required to keep accurate records during the entire adoption process. Some of the most common complaints of returning adoptees include a lack of access to adoption records and discrepancies between the adoption records that they are given and the records that are kept at agencies. In the past, these discrepancies have occurred due to a lack of administrative standards or intentional falsification. In her speech, Trenka gave a list of eight types of these abuses, documented by TRACK in real-life cases.

One of these, for example, is a falsified "orphan hojuk." According to the adoption laws of many of the countries where children are sent, the child must be an orphan to be adopted. In order to create the illusion that the child was in fact an orphan—even in cases where children did have families and may have even appeared on their family hojuk (registry)—agencies created "orphan hojuks" to indicate that the child had no family, which is a falsification of a legal document. Trenka says her own case shows multiple examples of these abuses by adoption agencies.

Trenka states that while adoptions may look legal on paper, falsification of records to facilitate adoptions is what Professor David Smolin, an academic expert on international adoption, calls, "child laundering," where children are obtained or sent under false pretenses, but processed to have "legal" adoption papers.

Adoption agencies often use the privacy rights of the parent as a reason why information may not be disclosed, but unethical practices in the past may be another motivation to keep adoptees in the dark.

When adoptees come searching for their personal information, these fragmented or inaccurate records make it nearly impossible to track down biological family; the current rate of success is a mere 2.7 percent. Adoption agencies often use the privacy rights of the parent as a reason why information may not be disclosed, but unethical practices in the past may be another motivation to keep adoptees in the dark. The new adoption law proposed by the coalition would require the agencies to surrender all information, excluding any identifying personal information of the parent. In order to enforce the accuracy of adoption records and access to them, the new adoption law proposal stipulates that a central authority should be run by the government. This central authority would house all adoption records, give assistance to adoptees in birth-family searches, and be a watchdog of adoption agencies.

Other parts of the proposal include lowering the age that a child can give their consent to an adoption from 15 to 13 years of age, granting adoptees the right to keep their Korean citizenship, parenting education for prospective adoptive parents to prevent disrupted adoptions, and mandatory birth registration regulations to prevent child trafficking and secret domestic adoptions.

Currently Korea has no law regarding birth registration, so 97 percent of domestic adoption is done in secret, with adoptive parents listing the child as their biological child.

Raising Korean Children in Korea Is a Priority

In an interview, Eun Sung-ho, the director of the Family Support Division in the Ministry of Health and Welfare, emphasized the government's commitment to revamping the country's adoption laws, stating [there would be] continued talks and plans for another public hearing on the subject by the end of this year. He said it was a priority for his department to promote a bill that makes the adoption procedures more transparent and fair, while preventing cases of disrupted adoptions. "We have to make it a priority to raise Korean children in Korea."

Rep. Choi said that she anticipates some opposition to the bill, which could hit the floor of the National Assembly next year, from proponents of international adoption, such as adoption agencies and prospective adoptive parents, and from those who think that making birth registration mandatory will discourage domestic adoption.

This is Rep. Choi's first time working with Korean adoptee community groups, but [she] said that she appreciates that adoptee groups want to work to make positive changes in Korean society. She encourages adoptee groups who are compelled to activism. "If there is a problem that can affect the relationship between Korea and other countries, it's important to work together to make changes ... not everything can be changed by laws, but when we change laws, we begin to change society."

ASK representative Kim Stoker said it's important that adoptees speak up. "As a foreigner, people might wonder why I'd be interested in changing legislation in Korea. Well, I am an adoptee . . . (and) even though I don't hold Korean citizenship, I have lived in this country for more than 10 years. Once I heard that the Special Adoption Law in Korea was going to be revised . . . I knew that we as a community living here in Korea had to be involved. Our voices needed to be heard."

Update: The South Korean National Assembly passed "The Special Act Relating to Adoption" (Bill # 1812414) on June 29, 2011 with 188 votes in favor, 4 abstentions, and 0 votes opposed. The revised "Special Act on Adoption" was promulgated on August 4, 2011 and went into effect on August 5, 2012.

The European Court of Human Rights Supports the Rights of Same-Sex Couples to Adopt

Elizabeth Burleson

In the following viewpoint, Elizabeth Burleson argues that the European Court of Human Rights (ECHR) supports same-sex marriage and the rights of gay and lesbian couples to adopt. She demonstrates that the ECHR has consistently ruled against laws that discriminate on the basis of sexual orientation. Burleson concludes that children around the world, including the United States, would benefit if governments would follow the lead of the ECHR and recognize same-sex marriage and parenting. Burleson is a professor at the University of South Dakota School of Law.

As you read, consider the following questions:

1. According to the viewpoint, when and why was the European Court of Human Rights established?

2. What are three legal cases Burleson cites regarding same-sex family jurisprudence?

3. How many countries signed in 2008 a United Nations declaration decriminalizing homosexuality, according to the viewpoint?

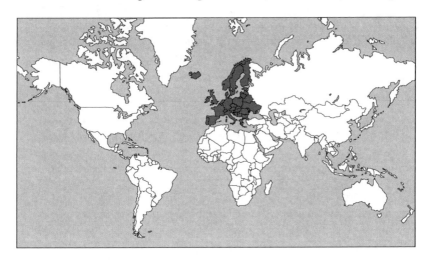

Currently, the European Court of Human Rights (ECHR) provides a model that other jurisdictions should consider in recognizing the legal status of same-sex families.

A country adopting another country's law as one's own legal system can upgrade or downgrade provisions for same-sex families. For example, "a same-sex marriage concluded in the Netherlands, Belgium, or Spain will be downgraded in England and Wales to a civil partnership, whereas a German eingetragene Lebenspartnerschaft will be upgraded in Belgium to a marriage" [according to scholar Katharina Boele-Woelki]. The ECHR protects the right to respect for family life, the right to marry, and the right not to be discriminated against on the basis of sex. Katharina Boele-Woelki calls for all jurisdictions to enhance the legal status of same-sex couples through a protocol adopted by the Hague Conference on Private International Law or through an international convention on the recognition of same-sex relationships.

In the meantime, gay and lesbian families look to the ECHR, which has held that member states are not permitted to discriminate on the basis of sexual orientation in adoption proceedings. Kathleen Doty notes that:

E.B. v. France has the potential to dramatically alter the landscape of gay and lesbian parental rights in Europe. By overruling *Fretté v. France*, the ECHR took a major step towards recognizing the full equality of gays and lesbians in Europe. Significantly, the case expands the applicability of Article 14 to the point of holding France, a nonsignatory, to the equality standards of Protocol 12. Additionally, in privileging the right to a private life free from discrimination over the national interest in protecting children, the ECHR narrowed the margin of appreciation it grants to States when it reviews State laws that have a discriminatory effect on gays and lesbians. While it remains to be seen what individual countries will do in response to *E.B. v. France*, the ECHR's decision sends a strong message to contracting States that provide rights to their citizens beyond those enumerated in the Convention: The provision of rights in a way that excludes gays and lesbians will not be tolerated.

The European Court of Human Rights Battles Discrimination

Located in Strasbourg, France, the ECHR was established in 1959 to hear cases brought pursuant to the Convention for the Protection of Human Rights and Fundamental Freedoms. Known as the European Convention on Human Rights (ECHR), the current system involves a permanent full-time court that came into operation on November 1, 1998. This permanent court superseded a two-tier, part-time court and commission. The court is competent to hear both interstate cases and individual applications, as long as domestic remedies have been exhausted. The court has the power to issue both advisory opinions and binding judgments, to which all contracting parties agree to abide. Modeled on the United Nations' [UN's] 1948 Universal Declaration of Human Rights, the Convention on Human Rights has been invoked to protect LGBT [lesbian, gay, bisexual, and transgender] people primarily through Articles 8 and 14. Article 8 provides that "[e]veryone has the right to respect for his private and family life, his home and his correspondence" while Article 14 prohibits discrimination "on any ground such as sex, race, colour, language, religion, political or other opinion, national or social origin, association with a national minority, property, birth or other status."

ECHR same-sex family jurisprudence builds upon several decades of case law dismantling discriminatory laws on the basis of sexual orientation. The European Court of Human Rights found in *Salgueiro da Silva Mouta v. Portugal* that a judge's denial of child custody to a gay father due to the father's sexual orientation was a discriminatory violation of privacy. In 2004, the court in *Fretté v. France* refrained from recognizing a gay man's right to adopt a child under the ECHR. Several years later in *E.B. v. France*, the court used the best interests of the child principle to hold that, "in rejecting the applicant's application for authorization to adopt, the domestic authorities made a distinction based on considerations regarding her sexual orientation, a distinction which is not acceptable under the Convention." Between the *Fretté* and *E.B.* decisions, the European scientific community clarified that gay parenting was healthy and deserved support.

The Development of Antidiscrimination Laws

In the years between *Fretté* and *E.B. v. France*, ECHR antidiscrimination law developed substantially. In particular, Protocol 12 now provides a widespread prohibition on discrimination while Article 7 of a new European Convention on the Adoption of Children recognizes a much broader notion of family than when *Fretté* was decided. While it had been opened for signature several years prior to the final decision in *Fretté*, Protocol 12 did not come into force until 2005. It is important to note that Protocol 12 is a much broader antidiscrimination provision than Article 14. The latter prohibits discrimi-

Gay Adoption Around the World

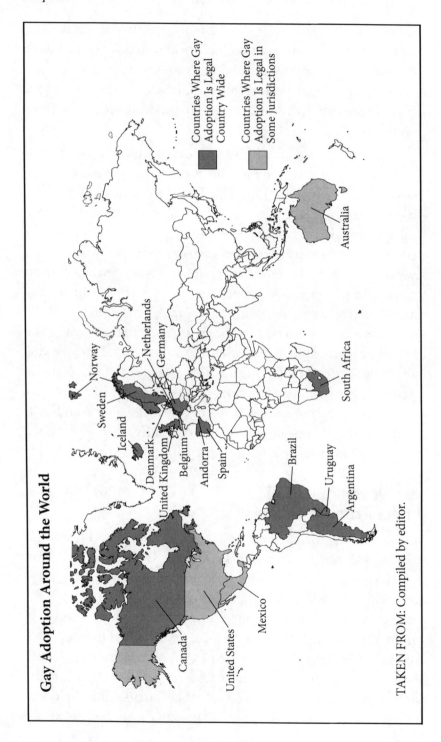

TAKEN FROM: Compiled by editor.

nation in relation to a right under the convention while Protocol 12 prohibits discrimination in relation to any right recognized by member states that accede to the protocol. Another important development was the Council of Europe's formation of a Working Group on Adoption, which has led to a revised European Convention on the Adoption of Children that is open for signature. Article 7 explains that countries can extend the scope of the convention to different or same-sex couples living together in a stable relationship or to individuals. *E.B. v. France* cites the European Convention on the Adoption of Children, further strengthening support for same-sex families. . . .

ECHR same-sex family jurisprudence builds upon several decades of case law dismantling discriminatory laws on the basis of sexual orientation.

Children Will Benefit

Children would benefit substantially if governments broadly recognized same-sex marriages and parenting. In the U.S., same-sex married partners soon will be counted in the census for the first time. The *Economist* notes "the 2010 census will provide the federal government's first official recognition of gay marriage, which is legal in six states. Past censuses have not reported data on gays." Internationally, information is even scarcer. United Nations High Commissioner for Human Rights, Navi Pillay, lamented that ten countries still have laws making homosexual activity punishable by death, explaining "[t]hose who are lesbian, gay or bisexual, those who are transgender, transsexual or intersex, are full and equal members of the human family and are entitled to be treated as such."

There has been significant progress in recognizing LGBT rights. In December 2008 sixty countries signed a UN declaration to decriminalize homosexuality. In July 2009, the Delhi High Court in India struck down its gay-sex ban. Yet the daily lives of millions of people are impacted by the legal invisibility of LGBT identity and discrimination. Children remain the silent victims of this widespread ambivalence. The time has come to recognize and support same-sex families.

Gay Canadian Women Encounter Difficulty in Exercising Their Right to Adopt

Meghan Davidson Ladly

In the following viewpoint, Meghan Davidson Ladly discusses adoption in Canada by lesbian, bisexual, and transgender (LBT) women. Although many adoptions in Canada are international, LBT women are having an increasingly difficult time accomplishing such adoptions, according to Ladly. The value system of sending countries often interferes with the process; only the United States allows openly LBT women to adopt. Consequently, LBT women sometimes choose to hide their sexuality when they interact with social workers concerning adoption, according to the author. Ladly is a British journalist who writes for the Canadian magazine This.

As you read, consider the following questions:

1. How many foreign children are adopted in Canada each year, according to the viewpoint?
2. How many contracting states are signatories to the 1993 Hague Convention on Protection of Children and Co-Operation in Respect of Intercountry Adoption?

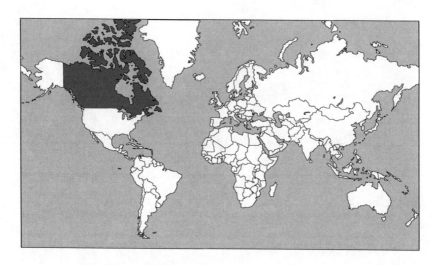

3. From where did Lisa adopt a baby girl in 2005?

The test kitchen of the Bayview Village Loblaws grocery store in North Toronto is packed. Around 30 women and men sit clustered in pairs in a horseshoe, framed by the cupboards and counters lining the room. They are almost all white, aged 30 to 60 years old. Some small houseplants sit on the counter, the floor is the colour of cream of carrot soup, and the cupboards are dark green; the aesthetic is vaguely grade school. Orchestral pop floats in from the grocery store, while outside the window, one floor below, shoppers select their salad greens. Some of the couples talk quietly amongst themselves. Others wait silently with an air of anticipation. No one is here for a cooking lesson.

A cheery woman in an argyle sweater takes up her position in the centre of the chairs and begins to speak. Welcome to "How to Adopt." This seminar, hosted by the Adoption Council of Ontario [ACO], is Adoption 101 for prospective parents interested in the idea but unsure where to start. The class outlines the various types of adoption and introduces attendees to parents who have gone through with adoption and who can speak about their personal experiences.

Three Types of Adoption in Ontario

There are three types of adoption in Ontario: public, private and international. ACO executive director Pat Convery stresses that each kind of adoption offers its own challenges and rewards, and the route a couple or individual chooses to pursue depends on their own personal situation. What she does not say, however, is that some personal situations affect the available options more than others.

Growing up in her home country of Iran, Shirin never imagined she would find herself in this situation. For many years, Iran promoted the virtues of large families. Shirin herself has many siblings. But now the Iranian government is thwarting her maternal ambitions. Shirin now lives in Canada and wants to adopt an Iranian child, but her birth country has declared her unfit. She came to the ACO meeting to learn about her adoption options, but unlike the couples here tonight, Shirin faces an additional obstacle. According to many countries, including Iran, she's an unacceptable candidate because she's gay.

Shirin is just one of an increasing number of queer women to pursue the option of international adoption, only to find that most countries classify them as substandard parents. Single mothers and lesbian couples disproportionately face barriers to international adoption because, not being in a heterosexual marriage, they're classified as single parents. Many countries explicitly state they will not allow single women, or gays and lesbians, to adopt children, favouring a family structure that includes a mother and father. While some countries do allow single women to adopt, no other country among those usually sourced for foreign adoption, with the exception of the United States, permits openly gay women to parent their children.

International adoption is popular in Canada, with Canadian citizens and permanent residents adopting around 2,000 foreign children each year. Canadians apply to private adoption agencies licensed by specific countries to place children with parents here. Of the three types of adoption, international adoptions are the most expensive, costing parents $25,000 to $50,000 per child. The $85 that couples pay to attend sessions like the Adoption Council seminar is just the beginning. Every prospective parent must undergo a "home study"—a series of in-home evaluations by adoption practitioners to ensure the applicants will be prepared and competent parents—as well as complete the mandatory adoptive parents training course known as PRIDE (Parent Resources for Information, Development and Education). While the Children's Aid Society does not charge for these services, many individuals opt to pay the thousands of dollars it costs to go through private agencies, because it cuts down on wait times.

Many countries explicitly state they will not allow single women, or gays and lesbians, to adopt children, favouring a family structure that includes a mother and father.

The Popularity of International Adoption

For many Canadians, the expense is worth it. International adoptions are popular because younger children are more readily available; at the very least there is a perception that kids up for adoption through the Children's Aid Society may be older, part of a sibling group, or have special needs. With private adoptions, there is the risk that a birth mother will change her mind and an adoptive parent's money and effort will be spent in vain. International adoption provides prospective parents with a formulaic stability. There is lots of paperwork, months of waiting, and usually travel abroad, but the path to parenthood is clear and understandable. Parental age is another factor: Women who delayed having families, whether to pursue careers or for any other reason, face barriers within the domestic adoption process that can often be avoided with international adoption. Women over 50 are unlikely to be given an infant domestically, for instance, but several countries, such as Bulgaria, have higher parental age limits for infant adoption. Some women, such as Shirin, have a connection to a certain country or region and would like to adopt a child from that part of the world. For all these reasons, international adoption is an important option—and for many, it is a last resort after the domestic adoption process fails. Yet a growing subset of potential parents is being excluded by the countries where Canadians adopt from most. Almost one-quarter of all children within Canada adopted internationally in 2008 came from China—a country that only permits heterosexual couples to adopt.

Many lesbian, bisexual, and trans [transgender (LBT)] women dismiss international adoption, because of its near impossibility for them and also because they object to their sexual orientation being treated as a liability. Some queer women, however, view these discriminatory policies as just one more problem they have to solve in order to adopt. These women opt instead to conceal their sexual orientation and go through the rigorous application procedures closeted, and in many cases they successfully adopt children from countries that discriminate against LGBT [lesbian, gay, bisexual, and transgender] individuals.

As for Shirin's plan, she is unsure of her options. She is a tall, fit woman with rich brown eyes and a few smile lines around her mouth. She has a discernible accent when she speaks. Shirin looks younger than she is, but in her late thirties she knows her options for adoption are narrowing. "I never admitted it to my family," she says, "but I want to have children." She wants a baby, preferably a healthy one, and while a child from the Middle East is no longer a possibility, there are still other alternatives open to her. Shirin does have one advantage; she may be gay—but she is also single.

The 1993 Hague Convention

There are 83 contracting states to the 1993 Hague Convention on Protection of Children and Co-operation in Respect of Intercountry Adoption. In the nearly two decades since the agreement was concluded, it has had a profound influence on international adoption for LBT women.

Designed to safeguard the interests of children and to combat child trafficking, the convention has changed how countries regulate adoption in several significant ways. Under the convention, keeping children within their own families or countries is prioritized. Foreign adoption is considered a last resort, to be taken only when all other domestic options have been exhausted.

Many lesbian, bisexual, and [transgender] women dismiss international adoption . . . because they object to their sexual orientation being treated as a liability.

"It's taken away some of the worries that adopting families would have," says Pat Convery, meaning that certain key questions are answered: "Was this child actually legally relinquished? Did the parent have every opportunity to parent the child? Did they really look to make sure there were no family members? Was there for sure no money that changed hands in those areas that would be illegal under Canadian law?"

But while the Hague convention has been a positive measure for intercountry adoption in general, it has also made it more difficult for queer women to adopt. The U.S., as the only source country that permits openly queer parents to adopt, used to be a haven for many LGBT and non-LGBT would-be adoptive parents. Since signing onto the Hague convention, however, more emphasis has been placed on securing domestic adoption for American children in need of homes.

Value Systems Impose Barriers to Adoption

More than the Hague convention, however, it is countries' own value systems that pose the largest obstacles to queer Canadians adopting abroad. Chris Veldhoven is the queer parenting programs coordinator at the 519 Church Street Community Centre in Toronto, and he teaches a seminar to would-be fathers entitled Daddies & Papas 2B that explores the topic of adoption among other parenting models and family creation practices.

"The screening tools for some countries are becoming more explicitly heterocentric," says Veldhoven, "so it's much more difficult for people to find a country that will officially welcome someone and not discriminate on sexual orientation or gender identity."

Historically, Veldhoven says, lesbians led the queer community in adopting, but increasingly gay male couples are also looking to adopt. Despite domestic legal victories that prevent discrimination on the basis of sexual orientation, there remains a stigma surrounding single men (or "single" men) adopting kids. Within intercounty adoption, this stigma is magnified. Single women may find their international adoption choices limited, but their situation is still better than that of single men—few countries even consider male applicants. . . .

Paradoxically, as social equality for LGBT individuals has strengthened within Canada, international adoption has become more difficult for queer women. Adoption practitioners who conducted the home studies of lesbian or bisexual women 10 or 15 years ago might have been willing to take a "Don't Ask, Don't Tell" attitude; if they thought someone would make a good parent, they could opt to keep a parent's sexual orientation out of their home study report. That's significantly less likely to be the case today.

"If you're going to be out and you have to have your home study done by a domestic social worker, they're not as willing to censor anymore because of the ethics of it," says Veldhoven. "In the face of decreased homophobia domestically, social workers are saying, 'Now we have to be true about your family configuration because we don't want to hide it, because you shouldn't have to hide it.' But for many countries internationally you do hide it."

Paradoxically, as social equality for [lesbian, gay, bisexual, and transgender] individuals has strengthened within Canada, international adoption has become more difficult for queer women.

The Importance of the Home Study

The process of the home study itself has also changed considerably over the last decade. Jackie Poplack is a social worker who has been working in the field for four decades and has been an adoption practitioner, which includes conducting home studies, for the last 14 years. According to Poplack, home studies have become much more standardized and involve a lot more verification than they used to. Poplack has worked with queer couples seeking children and says that for social workers, looking the other way is not an option. "I'm going to be 100 percent honest and if I have a question or concern I say it," she says. But for prospective parents who are single, there's a certain degree of plausible deniability. In her years as a practitioner, Poplack has had one or two clients who said they were heterosexual, and who might have believed that themselves, but who she thought could have been gay. When it comes to home studies, she acknowledges that, regardless of sexuality, people will try and smooth over any aspects of their character that they think will diminish their chances of securing a child.

Lisa is one woman who hid it. In 2005, she adopted a baby girl from Haiti. She was closeted to her social worker, so the woman classified her as heterosexual on her home study report. Lisa was single, so while there were some fridge magnets to remove and books to hide, there was no life partner to implausibly pass off as a roommate. Today she is wearing blue jeans and an olive T-shirt with "garden hoe" written across it in black letters. As she sits sipping her mug of coffee, she smiles, talking about the process of adopting her daughter, who arrived in Canada at nine months old and who is now happily enrolled in grade school with no idea of the half-truths her mother told to secure her.

"My goal was to never lie," says Lisa, picking her words carefully. "But not necessarily to say everything."

The Sherbourne Health Centre sits at 333 Sherbourne Street in downtown Toronto, a massive structure of glass and concrete with wood accents elevated from the road. Across the street is Allan Gardens. People sit on benches and soak up the sun by the greenhouse. Squirrels play in the bare branches of the trees and scurry up the wrought iron lampposts that dot the grounds. Rachel Epstein's office is on the second floor of the centre. Epstein is coordinator of the LGBTQ Parenting Network at the centre. The parenting course she designed, Dykes Planning Tykes, has been running since 1997.

In Epstein's years of experience working with queer parents, she has seen women closet themselves and get children. But today she is more pessimistic about the possibilities for LBT women to adopt from abroad.

"Basically, queers do not see international adoption as an option," she says. More countries are selective about who adopts and who doesn't, and choose heterosexual married couples over single individuals. Epstein worries about the personal toll exacted by denying your sexuality. "In the past, either you are single or you closet yourself. You closet your relationship," says Epstein. "I mean, even single people find it hard to go closeted for this process, and it can be not just the adoption process but for a while afterwards."

The Role of the Social Worker

For a potential LBT parent, finding a social worker to whom she can be open about her sexuality—and who is willing to omit her sexual orientation from the home study report—is rare. How open a woman will be with her social worker is a crucial decision that can set her adoption back months if the wrong choice is made. If a woman chooses to be honest and the social worker is unwilling to lie, then the woman must find another social worker and start the process again. "It's more feasible if you're single," says Epstein. "You don't get defined by your sexual orientation in the same way and it's easier to not talk about that."

Indeed, there are those within Canada's tight-knit LGBT adoption community who feel that the less said about queers and international adoption the better. Many blame U.S. media coverage of queer adoptive parents as being instrumental in China's decision to ban single women from adopting. As awareness of the issue grows in diplomatic circles, they say, more consulates close their doors, shutting off the few remaining channels available for women seeking this route to parenthood. One Canadian adoption advocate refused to be interviewed for this [viewpoint] and strongly discouraged publishing any story at all on the subject.

There are no easy answers to a problem of such emotional, legal, and cultural complexity. For Canadian social workers, having to lie about sexual orientation in a home study report is a serious dilemma. "That's unethical; I would never do that," says Poplack. "It's tough sometimes, because some of the rules you think are really unfair. I think we have to respect other countries—but it's really crappy for gays and lesbians."

Lisa made the decision to out herself to her adoption practitioner after her adoption was finalized and, as a social worker herself, she has spent a long time thinking about the ethical implications of her decision. "How do you reconcile that you are going against our [Canadian] Charter of Rights and Freedoms? Okay, it is the other country's rules—but they're homophobic and they go against our codes. Social workers haven't been able to work it out in a way that enables most of them to feel comfortable," says Lisa. "So the people who are doing it are like the people who work as social workers for Catholic Charities and then pass condoms out under the table; they're basically doing it very quietly, very silently, afraid themselves to come out."

For a potential [lesbian, bisexual, or transgender] parent, finding a social worker to whom she can be open about her sexuality . . . is rare.

To Lie or Not to Lie

The Loblaws seminar draws to a close. Everyone stands to put on their coats, wrapping scarves around their necks. The music drifting in from the grocery store has changed to the Beach Boys. Shirin thinks she may not adopt. "I can't lie about this fact," she says. "The home study is going to be really one-to-one, close work between me and the social worker or case worker, and that is going to be based on trust. The person should know about me, should know about my past, should know about my family, should know about everything. How is it going to be possible to not say such a big fact?"

She'll do some more research and talk to a friend who is also looking into intercountry adoption, but she's still skeptical. Shirin did not come out as gay until later in her life, and after being closeted for so long she doesn't want to be in that situation again. "I don't approve of it; to lie about it," she says. "You should be honest."

Lisa, however, is contemplating adopting another child from Haiti. She will need to find a new social worker, one who doesn't know she's gay. Then she'll undergo another home study, closeted again, but she's willing to do it for another child. "I think I'm a seasoned pro now at it," she says. "I've guided other people about how to do it; I can do it myself again and I've been through it once so it's not as scary." When she thinks back to the emotional toll of concealing her sexuality the first time, she reflects, "I never really lost connection to who I was as a person; I was just playing the game."

It is a game that Shirin and countless other queer women may simply decide not to play.

Sharia Law in Pakistan Does Not Allow the Transfer of Parental Rights to Adoptive Parents

Australian Government Migration Review Tribunal

In the following viewpoint, the Australian Government Migration Review Tribunal offers advice to people hoping to adopt a child from Pakistan. Because sharia law, a law practiced in many Islamic countries, does not permit parental rights to be transferred to non-related individuals, customary adoption is not generally recognized. At issue is the obscuring of the child's identity by the severing of his or her ties with birth parents. However, guardianships and wardships are available forms of care for children who have no parents to care for them. In addition, Islam provides for an additional form of alternative care called kafala.

As you read, consider the following questions:

1. What does the alternative form of care called *kafala* entail? What does a person entering this agreement pledge to do?

2. Under what convention does the United Nations recognize *kafala*?

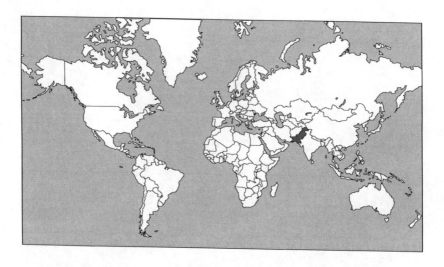

3. What is the difference between de jure and de facto guardianship in Pakistan?

Pakistan's legal system is based on the *shariah* [Islamic law] which does not recognise adoption in the legal sense—that is, to establish a parent-child relationship between individuals who are not related by blood. Consequently, there is no statutory provision for adoption in Pakistan. The following excerpt from *The Politics of Adoption* [by Kerry O'Halloran] explains the tension between adoption and Islam:

> Islam does not, strictly speaking, recognize the term 'adoption'. In most Islamic states, adoption as it is known in Western nations is impossible. Any process that purports to alter family genealogy, to change the authentic identity of an individual and potentially disadvantage 'legitimate' children, is generally frowned upon in Muslim culture. Adoption in particular is anathema as it involves the permanent and absolute transfer of parental rights to adoptive parents, a denial of ancestry and falsifying of bloodlines.

Guardianship vs. Adoption

Despite this, Pakistan law enables children to be placed under the guardianship of a suitable individual—as an alternative means of care. In 1994, the Pakistan government provided the following information concerning in-country adoptions, and the situation appears to remain current:

> Adoption is not governed by any law in Pakistan/Islam. It does not mean that adoption is literally prohibited in Pakistan. Children in especial circumstances are placed under the guardianship of their near relatives or suitable person appointed by court. In that case the children do not automatically adopt the parentage of their guardians. They will legally enjoy all social and economic rights except for inheritance of property from their guardian.

The Concept of *Kafala*

In Pakistan, *kafala* defines a system of alternative care that could be considered a form of customary adoption. It provides a model of alternative care that—unlike legal adoption—preserves the blood ties between the child and its biological parents—an acceptable practice under Islam. An excerpt from *The Politics of Adoption* provides a definition of *kafala*:

> *Kafala* is an Arabic legal term for a formal pledge to support and care for a specific orphaned or abandoned child until he or she reaches majority. A form of unilateral contract, it is used in various Islamic nations to assure protection for such minors, as these nations generally do not legally recognize the concept of adoption.

Under *kafala*, children are placed under the guardianship of an individual—always the male in the case of a married couple—through either an informal or formal arrangement:

> In Islam what can be termed adoption is at best an alternative care arrangement for a child whose parents have died or are unable to provide the necessary physical care, love and protection. Such children are then cared for by a set of parents or guardians who act as caregivers with the consent,

whether written or verbal, from the natural parents or next of kin. Natural parents do not give up their parental rights. Instead, by mutual agreement, they make care arrangements with others for the upbringing of their child.

Importantly, under *kafala*, adopted children have no inheritance rights and typically do not take on the family surname. This is due to the primacy Islam places on family relationships, parentage and lineage. However, adoptive parents may bequeath property rights on their adopted children, according to O'Halloran:

> Islam places great importance upon respecting the inviolable integrity of the 'natural' family unit. While he or she [the child] has no inherent legal rights of inheritance in relation to their adopters, the latter may make arrangements during their lifetime to confer property rights on their adopted children.

[Kafala] provides a model of alternative care that— unlike legal adoption—preserves the blood ties between the child and its biological parents—an acceptable practice under Islam.

Kafala appears to take place without the state involvement in certain circumstances, for example between members of an extended family. Put by O'Halloran:

> By far the majority of adoptions in Islamic states take the form of informal, long-term, first-party, care arrangements (or *kafala*) within the child's extended family and, as there are no placement rights as such, the parties are essentially left to their own devices. In third-party domestic adoptions, where all rights in respect of the orphan or abandoned child are vested in the designated government agency, the placement procedure is controlled by that agency.

The Role of Adoption in Islam

There are often misconceptions about the role of adoption in Islam. The fact is that the Islamic form of "adoption" is called *kafala*, which literally means sponsorship, but comes from the root word meaning "to feed." It is best translated as "foster parenting." Algerian family law defines the concept thusly: "*Kafala*, or legal fostering, is the promise to undertake without payment the upkeep, education and protection of a minor, in the same way as a father would do for his son".

Pakistan Adoption,
"Adoption Facts: What Islam Says About Adoption?," 2011.
www.pakistanadoption.com.

Kafala is also a practice that has UN [United Nations] recognition under the Convention on the Rights of the Child, to which Pakistan is a signatory. . . .

Guardians and Wards Act

The Guardians and Wards Act, 1890 (originally promulgated under the British system) is relevant to customary adoption in that it formalises the guardian-ward relationship. . . .

The act enables an individual to obtain legal guardianship of a child (a practice consistent with *kafala* but not mandatory). All sources appear to indicate that *kafala* can be done in conjunction with the state, but this is probably more common when an orphanage or third party is involved.

To obtain legal guardianship, an application must be submitted to the relevant district court for consideration.

Despite the availability of this process, the practice of *kafala* does not appear to stipulate a requirement to legalise guardianship. Moreover, O'Halloran notes that in 'Islamic countries, most domestic adoptions are first-party informal care arrangements or *kafala*, and are not necessarily endorsed by court orders.' Jillani & Associates—a Pakistan-based law firm specialising in family law—also provides the following information:

> A guardian can be a de facto or a de jure one. Legal guardians and those appointed by the court are de jure guardians. A father is the natural guardian of a child under the age of 18 years under the GWA [Guardians and Wards Act, 1890].

> As opposed to a de jure guardian, a person, like the mother, brother, uncle, other relations except father and father's father, or an institution like an orphanage, may voluntarily place himself or herself in charge of the person or property of the minor; a mother, however, is the next possible guardian after a father, unless the latter, by his will, has appointed another person as the guardian of the child. She under certain circumstances can appoint a guardian by will. She can do so during the lifetime of her husband if he is incapable of acting; or after his death. A de facto guardian, as opposed to a de jure guardian, is merely a custodian of the person and property of the minor.

Consequently, it would be reasonable to expect that not all 'adoptions' are formalised in Pakistan. However, there is no information to indicate the extent to which either de jure or de facto guardianship is practised, nor is there any information to indicate which is preferred.

Large families do give up 'spare' children for overseas adoption and . . . Pakistan courts have agreed to such arrangements in the past.

Fostering Is Encouraged

Relevant to the applicant, O'Halloran has provided some additional information on adoptions in Pakistan, indicating that the circumstances surrounding this particular case are not unique:

Fostering, in theory, is positively encouraged because it does not involve any transfer of parental rights nor does it obscure a child's identity. Indeed, there is always the possibility of such children being fostered by nonrelatives. Childless couples (even foreign Muslim childless couples) may take in a child from an orphanage, or a 'spare' child from a large family, and then later, in another country, may adopt that child. In Pakistan, for example, as long as the child is to be brought up as a Muslim, the courts will agree to such arrangements and will give permission for the child to be taken abroad.

Although in this case, the adoptive parents are related, the information at least indicates that large families do give up 'spare' children for overseas adoption and that Pakistan courts have agreed to such arrangements in the past.

Periodical Bibliography

The following articles have been selected to supplement the diverse views presented in this chapter.

Kathryn Blaze Carlson	"Your Baby Is Dead: Mothers Claim Their Supposedly Stillborn Babies Were Stolen from Them," *National Post* (Ontario), March 24, 2012.
Judy Cooper	"Identity Theft by Another Name? Is It Fair to Change the Forename of Adopted Children or Does It Erode Their Identity?," *Community Care*, September 16, 2010.
Carol Coulter	"New Law May Allow Children of Married Parents to Be Adopted," *Irish Times* (Dublin), January 30, 2012.
Giuliana Fuscaldo and Sarah Russell	"Potential Parents Put Through the Wringer in Their Attempt to Adopt a Child," *Age* (Sydney), November 4, 2010.
David Holmes	"'Adoption Is No Longer a Secret to Be Swept Under the Carpet,'" *Independent* (London), November 2, 2010.
Kate Holmquist	"'Why I Chose Adoption over an Abortion,'" *Irish Times* (Dublin), November 8, 2010.
Ron Nixon	"An Unfolding Sense of Identity; South Korean Adoptees from Decades Ago Share Struggle to Find True Self," *International Herald Tribune* (France), November 10, 2009.
Kirsty Taylor	"Korean Adoptees Raise Cash So Moms Can Keep Their Kids," *Korea Herald* (Seoul), November 23, 2011.
Cheryl Wetzstein	"Study: Families Trending Toward Open Adoption," *Washington Times*, March 21, 2012.

For Further Discussion

Chapter 1

1. What are some of the major problems associated with the process of adoption in various countries around the world, and how are governments attempting to address these problems, according to the viewpoints in this chapter?

2. What trends are emerging concerning the number of adoptions and the characteristics of adoption around the world, according to the viewpoints in this chapter?

Chapter 2

1. What is the Hague convention on intercountry adoption, and how does its enactment affect transnational adoption, according to several viewpoints in this chapter?

2. What are some of the dangers of transnational adoption, especially concerning child trafficking, according to the viewpoints in this chapter?

Chapter 3

1. Several of the viewpoints in this chapter claim that Australian Aboriginal, American Indian, and Canadian First Nations babies were taken from their families and placed for adoption. When did this happen, and what have nations done to recompense the damage? What explanations are offered for the adoption of these children by white couples?

2. Using the viewpoints in this chapter as evidence for your opinion, do you think that children should be placed in same-race families for adoption, or should adoptions be "color-blind"?

Chapter 4

1. Do you think that adult adoptees should have the right to their birth records, or do you believe that all adoption records should be sealed to preserve the privacy of birth parents? Explain, using the viewpoints in this chapter as evidence to support your point of view.

2. What kinds of problems do same-sex couples face when they attempt to adopt children either domestically or internationally, according to the viewpoints in this chapter?

Organizations to Contact

The editors have compiled the following list of organizations concerned with the issues debated in this book. The descriptions are derived from materials provided by the organizations. All have publications or information available for interested readers. The list was compiled on the date of publication of the present volume; the information provided here may change. Be aware that many organizations take several weeks or longer to respond to inquiries, so allow as much time as possible.

Adoptive Families
39 W. Thirty-Seventh Street, 15th Floor, New York, NY   10018
(646) 366-0830 • fax: (646) 366-0842
e-mail: letters@adoptivefamilies.com
website: www.adoptivefamilies.com

Adoptive Families publishes the award-winning American adoption magazine *Adoptive Families*. Much of the magazine is available online. In addition, the organization's website offers links to articles and information on a wide range of resources including foster adoption, transracial adoption, and older child adoption. The organization's website also provides an adoption guide and an adoption directory.

British Association for Adoption and Fostering (BAAF)
Saffron House, London   EC1N 8TS
    United Kingdom
(020) 7421-2600 • fax: (020) 7421-2601
e-mail: mail@baaf.org.uk
website: www.baaf.org.uk

The British Association for Adoption and Fostering (BAAF) is an advocacy organization that works for the best outcome for children in the foster care system. BAAF works to find families for these children and advise law and policy makers, as well as provide information to the general public about adoption. In addition to an adoption blog and resources for helping adoptees locate their birth parents, the BAAF website includes a long list of publications, including a catalog of books and resources for children and young people.

Center for Adoption Policy (CAP)
168A Kirby Lane, Rye, NY 10580
website: www.adoptionpolicy.org

The Center for Adoption Policy (CAP) believes that "ethical and effective legislation and policy create families." The organization provides research, analysis, advice, and education about current legislation and practices governing adoption in the United States and internationally. The organization's website includes descriptions of ethical adoption, facts and figures, and government bulletins.

Child Welfare Information Gateway
Children's Bureau/ACYF, Washington, DC 20024
(800) 394-3366
e-mail: info@childwelfare.gov
website: www.childwelfare.gov

The Child Welfare Information Gateway is the government agency whose mission is to promote "the safety, permanency, and well-being of children, youth, and families by connecting child welfare, adoption, and related professionals as well as the general public" to resources and information on topics related to the welfare of children. The agency's website provides information on all aspects of adoption, including the history of adoption, ethical issues concerning adoption, and legal concerns in the adoption process.

Children's Home Society and Family Services (CHSFS)
1605 Eustis Street, St. Paul, MN 55108
(651) 646-7771
website: www.chsfs.org

The Children's Home Society and Family Services (CHSFS) is a not-for-profit adoption organization that works "to give every child security, opportunity and a loving family," according to its website. The organization believes that a family is every child's most basic human right. The organization's publications include *Today's Child & Family* newsletter, which is available on its website, as well as a blog and Facebook page.

Dave Thomas Foundation for Adoption
716 Mount Airyshire Boulevard, Suite 100
Columbus, OH   43235
(800) 275-3832
e-mail: info@davethomasfoundation.org
website: www.davethomasfoundation.org

The Dave Thomas Foundation for Adoption is an advocacy organization devoted to increasing the number of adoptions of children in foster care in North America. To accomplish this, the organization provides adoption resources and information concerning adopting children from foster care. The organization sponsors the annual *A Home for the Holidays* television special aimed at raising money and awareness. The organization's website has brochures, posters, and resources available for free download.

Evan B. Donaldson Adoption Institute
120 E. Thirty-Eighth Street, New York, NY   10016
(212) 925-4089
e-mail: info@adoptioninstitute.org
website: www.adoptioninstitute.org

The Evan B. Donaldson Adoption Institute is a national not-for-profit organization whose mission is to "provide leadership that improves adoption laws, policies and practices—through sound research, education and advocacy—in order to better the lives of everyone touched by adoption." To this end, the organization conducts original research to provide solid information to lawmakers and stakeholders. It publishes the *Adoption Institute E-Newsletter*, fact sheets, and a comprehensive database of adoption research.

Origins Canada

Valerie Andrews, Executive Director
Richmond HillOntario   L4B 4R4
  Canada
(416) 400-5730
e-mail: contact@originscanada.org
website: www.originscanada.org

According to the group's website, Origins Canada is a volunteer nonprofit organization "serving people across Canada who have been separated from family members by adoption." The group believes that adoption causes emotional damage to both the adoptee and the birth family and that needless separation among family members should be eradicated. The website includes articles about adoption trauma and healing, coercive adoption, and historical studies about adoption. Origins Canada also publishes information concerning adoption and human rights as well as resources targeted for aboriginal peoples. Particularly interesting are articles and resources concerning the Sixties Scoop, the widespread adoption of indigenous children that began in the 1960s and continued into the 1980s.

United Nations Children's Fund (UNICEF)

UNICEF House, New York, NY   10017
(212) 326-7000
website: www.unicef.org

The United Nations Children's Fund (UNICEF) is the branch of the United Nations that works for the welfare of children around the globe. UNICEF upholds and promotes the human rights of children. The organization's website includes many articles about adoption, child trafficking, and intercountry adoption. In addition, UNICEF publishes fact sheets and statistics concerning adoption. The Convention on the Rights of the Child is an extensive document located on the website and is useful for students examining legal and ethical issues of adoption.

Bibliography of Books

David Brodzinsky and Adam Pertman — *Adoption by Lesbians and Gay Men: A New Dimension in Family Diversity.* New York: Oxford University Press, 2012.

Susan Caughman and Isolde Motley — *You Can Adopt: An Adoptive Families Guide.* New York: Ballantine Books, 2009.

Aaron Eske — *My Family, a Symphony: A Memoir of Global Adoption.* London: Palgrave Macmillan, 2010.

Karin Evans — *The Lost Daughters of China: Adopted Girls, Their Journey to America, and the Search for a Missing Past.* New York: Penguin, 2008.

Ann Fessler — *The Girls Who Went Away: The Hidden History of Women Who Surrendered Children for Adoption in the Decades Before Roe vs. Wade.* New York: Penguin, 2007.

Matthew L.M. Fletcher, Wenona T. Singel, and Kathryn E. Fort, eds. — *Facing the Future: The Indian Child Welfare Act at 30.* East Lansing: Michigan State University Press, 2009.

Abbie E. Goldberg — *Gay Dads: Transitions to Adoptive Fatherhood.* New York: New York University, 2012.

Susan Devan Harness	*Mixing Cultural Identities Through Transracial Adoption: Outcomes of the Indian Adoption Project (1958–1967)*. Lewiston, NY: Edwin Mellen Press, 2008.
Ellen Herman	*Kinship by Design: A History of Adoption in the Modern United States*. Chicago, IL: University of Chicago Press, 2008.
Eleana Jean Kim	*Adopted Territory: Transnational Korean Adoptees and the Politics of Belonging*. Durham, NC: Duke University Press, 2010.
Ellen Lewin	*Gay Fatherhood: Narratives of Family and Citizenship in America*. Chicago, IL: University of Chicago Press, 2009.
Betty Jean Lifton	*Lost & Found: The Adoption Experience*. Ann Arbor: University of Michigan Press, 2009.
Nancy McCabe	*Crossing the Blue Willow Bridge: A Journey to My Daughter's Birthplace in China*. Columbia: University of Missouri Press, 2011.
Barbara A. Moe	*Adoption: A Reference Handbook*. Santa Barbara, CA: ABC-CLIO, 2007.
Debra Monroe	*On the Outskirts of Normal: Forging a Family Against the Grain*. Dallas, TX: Southern Methodist University Press, 2010.

Elisabeth O'Toole *In on It: What Adoptive Parents Would Like You to Know About Adoption: A Guide for Relatives and Friends.* St. Paul, MN: Fig Press, 2011.

Adam Pertman *Adoption Nation: How the Adoption Revolution Is Transforming Our Families—and America.* Boston, MA: Harvard Common Press, 2011.

Barbara Bisantz Raymond *The Baby Thief: The Untold Story of Georgia Tann, the Baby Seller Who Corrupted Adoption.* New York: Da Capo Press, 2007.

Erin Siegal *Finding Fernanda: Two Mothers, One Child, and a Cross-Border Search for Truth.* Boston, MA: Beacon Press, 2012.

Deborah N. Silverstein and Susan Livingston Smith *Siblings in Adoption and Foster Care: Traumatic Separations and Honored Connections.* Westport, CT: Praeger, 2008.

Rita J. Simon and Sarah Hernandez *Native American Transracial Adoptees Tell Their Stories.* Lanham, MD: Lexington Books, 2008.

Darron T. Smith, Cardell K. Jacobson, and Brenda G. Juárez *White Parents, Black Children: Experiencing Transracial Adoption.* Lanham, MD: Rowman & Littlefield Publishers, 2011.

Rachael Stryker | *The Road to Evergreen: Adoption, Attachment Therapy, and the Promise of Family.* Ithaca, NY: Cornell University Press, 2010.

United Nations | *Child Adoption: Trends and Policies.* New York: United Nations, 2009.

Nancy Newton Verrier | *The Primal Wound: Understanding the Adopted Child.* London: BAAF, 2009.

Jacob R. Wheeler | *Between Light and Shadow: A Guatemalan Girl's Journey Through Adoption.* Lincoln: University of Nebraska Press, 2011.

Index

Geographic headings and page numbers in **boldface** refer to viewpoints about that country or region.

Rudd, Kevin, 130, 136, 139, 141, 145
Russia
  children adopted via international adoption, 24, 74, 74t, 79, 181–182
  international adoption stories, 70, 71–72, 79
  rates of adoption, 22, 26t
Rwanda, 91–92, 96

S

Salgueiro da Silva Mouta v. Portugal (Portugal; 1999), 193
Same-sex couples
  adoption rights, European Court of Human Rights, 190–196
  adoption rights/bans, 45–46, 120, *194*, 197, 199, 201, 206
  Canadian adoption challenges, 197–208
  international adoption, China, 75, 120, 201
  marriage rights, European Court of Human Rights, 191, 192
  marriage rights, global, 190, 195
Savelyev, Artyom, 70, 71–72
Scarth, Sandra, 53
Second daughters, China, 111, 114
Selman, Peter, 71–72
Servitude situations, 84, 88
Sex-selective abortion, 116, 118
Sexual abuse, 88, 92, 133–134
Sexual orientation, hiding, 197, 199, 201, 203–208
Shannon, Geoffrey, 81
Sharia law, 209–215
Single parenthood
  adoption bans, global, 120, 199, 206

adoption laws, global, 23, 27
  greater acceptance results in fewer adoptions, 16, 24–25, 172–173
  men, 203
  single gays, 199, 201, 203, 204–206
  support given, France, 185
  support needed, Korea, 179, 182–185
"Sixties Scoop" (Canada), 147, 148, 150
Smith, Merle, 142–143
Smolin, David, 103, 187
Smyth, Jamie, 77–83
So Ra Mi, 181
Social workers
  gay adoption, 203–205, 206–207
  international adoption, 72–73, 99, 100–101
  transracial adoption, 44–45, 153, 154–157
South Dakota, 123, 124, 125–126, 128–129
South Korea, 179–189
  See also Korea
Spain
  international adoption, 24, 112
  same-sex marriage, 191
Special Act Relating to Adoption (Korea; 2011), 188–189
State Supreme Courts, 165–166
Stepparents
  adoption by gender, 26–27
  adoption discouraged, 23, 24
  adoption rates, 24, 173
Sterilization programs, 114
Stevenson, Juliet, 94
Stoker, Kim, 189
"Stolen generations" (Aboriginal Australians), 15–16, 130–139, 140–145
Stringer, David, 152–157

3m